Love
IS MY SAVIOR

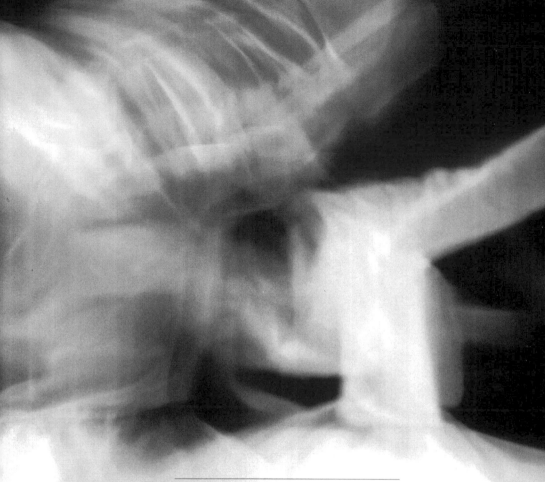

ARABIC LITERATURE AND LANGUAGE SERIES

The Arabic Literature and Language series serves to make available Arabic literature and educational material to the general public as well as academic faculty, students, and institutions in collaboration with local Arab writers from the region. The series will focus on publishing Arabic literature translated into English from less commonly translated regions of the Arab world and from genres representing vibrant social issues in Arabic literature. The series will make available poetry books in dual language (Arabic/English), novels, short stories, and anthologies. It will also publish textbooks for teaching Arabic language, literature, and culture, and scholarly works about the region.

Love IS MY SAVIOR

THE ARABIC POEMS OF RUMI

Translated and edited by
Nesreen Akhtarkhavari and **Anthony A. Lee**

Michigan State University Press • East Lansing

⊗ The paper used in this publication meets the minimum requirements
of ANSI/NISO z39.48-1992 (R 1997) (Permanence of Paper).

Michigan State University Press
East Lansing, Michigan 48823-5245

Printed and bound in the United States of America.

22 21 20 19 18 17 16   1 2 3 4 5 6 7 8 9 10

LIBRARY OF CONGRESS CATALOGING-IN-PUBLICATION DATA
Jalal al-Din Rumi, Maulana, 1207–1273.
[Poems. Selections. English]
Love is my savior : the Arabic poems / Rumi ;
translated by Nesreen Akhtarkhavari and Anthony A. Lee.
pages cm
English translations of 33 Arabic poems and fragments,
taken from the first 1010 poems in Rumi's Divan-e Shams.
Includes bibliographical references.
ISBN 978-1-61186-200-3 (pbk. : alk. paper)—ISBN 978-1-60917-486-6 (pdf)
ISBN 978-1-62895-261-2 (epub)—ISBN 978-1-62896-261-1 (kindle)
1. Jalal al-Din Rumi, Maulana, 1207–1273—Translations into English.
I. Akhtarkhavari, Nesreen, translator. II. Lee, Anthony A., 1947– translator. III. Title.
PK6480.E5A45 2016
891.'5511—dc23
2015017690

Book design by Sharp Des!gns, Lansing, Michigan
Cover design by Shaun Allshouse, www.shaunallshouse.com
Cover artwork is from an Ottoman-era manuscript depicting
Jalal al-Din Rumi and Shams-e Tabrizi.

Michigan State University Press is a member of the Green Press Initiative and is
committed to developing and encouraging ecologically responsible publishing
practices. For more information about the Green Press Initiative and the use
of recycled paper in book publishing, please visit www.greenpressinitiative.org.

Visit Michigan State University Press at www.msupress.org

CONTENTS

GOOD NEWS!

PREFACE

The poems of the thirteenth-century Islamic teacher, scholar, and poet, Muhammad Jalal al Din al-Balkhi, known to us as Rumi, have shaped Muslim culture for centuries. They still stand, after eight hundred years, as relevant and vital. Rumi speaks to us of unchanging spiritual realities and the universal quest for inner peace. His poems make a convincing argument for the central role of love, not only in Islamic texts and traditions, but in the consciousness of the human race. Rumi found in mystical poetry a vehicle for the expression of the endless spiritual bounties of love.[1] This became the center of his faith and practice and his connection with the Divine. He pronounced love to be the goal of his life and the only form of true worship. He demands the same of everyone.

> If you're not in love, you have missed your goal.
> He calls! The breeze of love must find your soul.
> Glory resurrected you, glory made you whole!
> If you're not in love, life has passed you by.[2]

The Realm of Love

Rumi's devotion to Shams-e Tabrizi (Arabic, literally translated as the Sun of Tabriz), also called Shams al-Din (literally translated as the Sun of Faith), is the central theme of his poetry. Rumi expresses his mystical passion for Shams, his guide and teacher, in joyful lines as a symbol of his love for God. Rumi's poems virtually pulsate with desire, longing, sensuality, and ecstatic celebration. His experiences of yearning, pain, lust, and joy flow out in timeless verse. These poetic visions move easily between dreams and real events, between internal states of luminosity and encounters with mundane external reality—always in a state of loving. However, to better understand Rumi's work, the reader should begin with some familiarity with his life and with the landscape of symbols and metaphors that inhabited his world. Only then can the deep meaning of Rumi's message be unveiled.

Rumi was born into a Muslim clerical family in 1207 CE, near the city of Balkh (in present-day northern Afghanistan) at the eastern edge of the Persian-speaking world.[3] His father, Baha al-Din Walad, was a revered Muslim scholar, theologian, and Sufi teacher. Rumi became his father's most diligent student and received a full classical, Islamic education. His family moved away from Balkh; wandered through Iran, the Arabian Peninsula, and Syria; and finally settled in Konya, in Anatolia (present-day Turkey). During these travels, Rumi met and learned from many Islamic scholars.

After the passing of his father in 1231 CE, Rumi was instructed for nine years by Sayed Burhan al-Din Muhaqiq Turmuthi, a scholar and Sufi and a student of his father's. Rumi spent five of these years in Syria, developing his Arabic and acquiring formal academic training. Upon his return from Syria, with the support of al-Turmuthi, Rumi started teaching in Konya and took over his father's position as the master of the Islamic school (*madrasa*). Assuming the normal duties of the learned class (*ulama*), Rumi preached in the mosque, taught in advanced religious circles, and gathered a large number of followers.

Yet, Rumi's mystical yearnings were not satisfied until he met Shams-e Tabrizi[4] on the afternoon of November 29, 1244—a date still celebrated by Sufi devotees today. The legends tell us that it was love at first sight. Despite the difference in age, upbringing, and social status, the two men found in one another the object of their spiritual quests: Shams, a mystic Sufi and a wandering scholar,[5] became Rumi's partner, companion, spiritual guide, and teacher.[6] Shams had searched all his life for a student who would be worthy of his knowledge and spiritual insight, whom he could teach the art of mystical love. He found his ideal student in Rumi.[7] Rumi became so engrossed in his sessions with Shams that he abandoned his duties at the teaching circles and in the mosque to spend all of his time with Shams. This became a source of alarm and resentment in the town, especially among Rumi's students. The students feared that this relationship, combined with Rumi's new Sufi practices, which included music and dance, might damage his reputation. They expressed these sentiments openly and showed their hostility toward Shams.

Then, without any warning, Shams left the city of Konya. Rumi was shocked and full of grief; he looked for Shams everywhere. Eventually, he heard that Shams was in Syria and sent his son, Sultan Walad, to Damascus to find him and bring him back. Shams returned to Konya, and Rumi arranged for him to marry a young woman in his household, Kimia Khatoon.[8] Meanwhile, Rumi resumed his sessions and close companionship with Shams, and the town's hostility toward Shams continued. About a year later, Kimia died. After that, Shams-e Tabrizi disappeared and was never heard from again. There are conflicting legends regarding this disappearance. Some presume that he left to continue his own spiritual quest in other lands, and others suggest that he was killed by Rumi's jealous students.[9]

Rumi was devastated, paralyzed with grief. For years, he searched for Shams, hoping to bring him back to Konya, but he never found him. In his inconsolable bereavement, Rumi expressed his thoughts and emotions in poetry. It was only after his separation from Shams that poems erupted from his spirit with intensity. In his poems, he tells about the agony that burned his soul.[10] Rumi eventually realized that his love for Shams was a token of an everlasting love, an eternal light inside him that obliterated the boundaries between all souls and connected all lovers to the Divine. He found some peace in this realization, and he was able to partially return to his clerical and teaching duties.

Meanwhile, Rumi continued to explore this new form spiritual practice. When Rumi became convinced that Shams was no longer alive, he took in a new companion and focal point for his inspiration: an old goldsmith friend, Salah al Din Faridun (Zarkub). After about ten years of companionship, Salah al-Din fell ill and died.[11] After that, Husam al-Din Akhi Tork, a younger scholar who knew and admired Rumi, dismissed his own students and dedicated himself to Rumi, becoming Rumi's new spiritual companion, scribe, and financial manager.[12] In Rumi's mind, his new companions were not meant to replace his beloved Shams-e Tabrizi, but were an extension of that love.

Husam al-Din convinced Rumi to allow him to write down his poems, sermons, and talks. Through Husam's diligent work, Rumi's writings were recorded and preserved. The long love poems (and a few quatrains) were collected in a volume that Rumi insisted on calling *Divan-e Shams-e Tabrizi*, meaning the collected poems of (or for, or by) Shams-e Tabrizi. Perhaps Rumi was attributing the inspiration for the poems to his teacher, perhaps he was suggesting that he and his teacher were one, or perhaps he simply wanted to ensure that the name of Shams-e Tabrizi would be permanently associated with the work.

The *Divan-e Shams-e Tabrizi*, like much of Rumi's work, is written mainly in Persian, but also includes Arabic and a few poems in Turkish and Greek. The poems in the divan are also of different types, with 3,283 long poems and 1,983 quatrains. These include poems that are fully Arabic (ninety long poems and nineteen quatrains). Arabic can also be found as full lines or as half-lines in many of the poems that are otherwise in Persian. Some are almost completely in Arabic, with the final line in Persian. Many poems have a number of lines in Arabic, with Persian verses preceding and following them.

Arabic is used in Rumi's other work as well. His epic manuscript *Masnavi* includes numerous single lines and longer passages that are entirely in Arabic. It is in the *Masnavi* that Rumi remarks that Arabic is sweeter than Persian, and then quickly adds that love has a hundred other languages.[13] This statement could be emphasizing the importance of Arabic as the language of Holy Text, but it also expresses Rumi's great respect for the language considered by many as the language of divinity.

Rumi's published lectures, or "Discourses," also include Arabic. One composition is entirely in Arabic, and another is all Arabic except for the first five words. In Rumi's "Sermons," there are short Arabic introductory prayers for each of the seven sermons. In addition, Arabic is also present in the rest of Rumi's work, including his "Letters." This is a testimony to Rumi's mastery and love for the language, a language he was fully versed in, as the vehicle of Islamic scholarship and discourse. But Rumi also enjoyed Arabic as the language of poetry and read the works of a number of Arabic classical poets.

The verses presented in this volume (complete odes and Arabic lines lifted from Persian poems) are beautiful, rhymed, and complementary to the concepts presented in his Persian poems. The difference in style and tone between his Arabic and Persian poems is dictated by the conventions of the two languages. It is obvious from reading the full poems that Persian and Arabic are intertwined to express a state of mind and being that does not recognize the boundaries of language.

Any reader of Rumi's divan will immediately realize that, in Persian and Arabic alike, Rumi sings only of love, which is the focus of his many compositions. In these poems, Rumi invokes his own all-consuming, burning, and tragic love for Shams-e Tabrizi—his teacher, friend, mystic guide, and lost beloved. Rumi is dissolved in the fire of love, a condition that other mystic poets who influenced him, including Sanai[14] and Attar,[15] also experienced and wrote about.

The Arabic Poems

Persian is an Indo-European language, different from Arabic, which is a root-based sematic language. Arabic is a Semitic language with different rules and linguistic forms. The mix of Arabic poems and lines in Rumi's Persian divan is a testimony to his mastery of Arabic, both Islamic and secular, and his competence in its poetic traditions, with their sophisticated structures. Rumi's beautiful, well-formed poems and eloquent prose are laden with religious, cultural, and literary allusions and idioms, as was (and still is) the practice in these traditions. Rumi was not only exposed to and influenced by Persian mystic poets, including Sanai[16] and Attar,[17] but he was also informed by the work of Arabic mystic and classical poets, including Al-Halaj,[18] Ibn Arabi,[19] and al-Mutanabbi.[20]

This book includes thirty-three Arabic poems and fragments, taken from the first 1010 poems in Rumi's *Divan-e Shams-e Tabrizi*. The poems have been translated directly from the original text of the divan and have been checked against Furuzanfar's edition of *Kulliyat Shams ya Divan-e Kabir*.[21]

The collection includes some poems written completely in Arabic and others that are sequences of Arabic lines embedded within Persian poems. Taking these lines and presenting them as independent poems is facilitated by the nature of Rumi's brilliant mind that, in every case, managed to construct the Arabic lines to represent complete thoughts or ideas. Upon examining the context in which the Arabic lines are related to the Persian poem as a whole, it becomes apparent that these lines complement the Persian verses by expanding, completing, or explaining thoughts, feelings, and spiritual realities expressed in the verses. As a scholar of Arabic, Rumi was aware that the language facilitates a wide range of conjugations, derivatives, and semantics. He made full use of the linguistic agility of the language, and sometimes even stretched words beyond their conventional boundaries to share a feeling or desire.

The Arabic poems in this collection display an aesthetic that complements Rumi's Persian poems and reflect his mastery of both Persian and Arabic. Although the structures of the poems in both languages are similar and Rumi pursues common themes in both, the Arabic poems are unique. This is partially a function of language. Arabic is a precise language with a wide range of vocabulary. Ideas are expressed clearly with powerful forms that sometimes sound harsh to Persian readers accustomed to the sweet melodies of a language full of decorative flourishes and cultural pleasantries. In the poems that combine Persian and Arabic verses, Rumi skillfully manages to create beautiful poems that seamlessly adhere to rhyme and meter in both languages.

The influence of Rumi's Islamic education and its role as the inspiration for his work is obvious through the extensive references to Islamic texts in his Arabic verses. He frequently uses the specific vocabulary of the Qur'an and images and expressions lifted from its verses. He also borrows from Islamic traditions and literature. Contemporary Sufi scholars who see Rumi as the Master of true Islamic thought and mystic philosophy have highlighted this background. They attribute his philosophy to his deep understanding of Islam and its teachings.[22] This influence is to be expected in light of Rumi's background, training, education, and profession. Rumi had studied Islam, memorized the Qur'an, and spent his life learning, teaching, and preaching Islamic texts. He was exposed to Sufi poetry and thoughts written mainly in Arabic. These, combined with his knowledge of ancient, classical philosophy, were obviously the source of his learning, though the main source was Islamic tradition. Consciously or unconsciously, he used them as a point of departure for his inspiration in both Arabic and Persian. This may be more obvious in the Arabic poems because the medium is the language of the Islamic sources Rumi was steeped in.

In Arabic, as in Persian, Rumi appears free to explore images of sexuality and desire, which are metaphors for spiritual longing. He uses images and expressions that usually are not well tolerated by his Persian readers. However, these expressions and images fit well within the Arabic literary tradition, accustomed as it is to explicit erotic imagery and language.

> So, honor me. Get drunk! Come here and be
> my companion. Radiant seeker! Come
> naked and embrace me. In earthly clothes
> you can't be saved or blessed with ecstasy.[23]

Rumi's Arabic verses are straightforward, and his metaphors are intense. The verses in this collection are as eloquent, metered,[24] smooth, and uninhibited as the Persian poems. It might be thought that in the Arabic we discover the free spirit of Rumi, unbound by polite and romantic traditions, free of formal conventions. Rumi seems to lose his inhibitions, willing to speak his mind and eager to share his unvarnished mystic insights. The poems flow from his consciousness, using the language that touches him at the moment of revelation.

The influence of Arab culture is also obvious in Rumi's work—a culture that is comfortable with sexuality as part of human nature. Perhaps, it is precisely his familiarity and competence in the language and culture that color his erotic images, even in the Persian poems. In his use of erotic language, Rumi was not breaking with Islamic texts or with Arabic poetic traditions, but was emulating and expanding those traditions to illustrate his spiritual mystic journey and attempt at self-annihilation in love—with all the joy, pain, and agony the experience produces.

The Erotic and the Homoerotic

Many of Rumi's poems appear, to the Western reader at least, to be surprisingly erotic. But those familiar with his poems will not be surprised to find frank and open expressions of physical love and sexual desire. The poet fully embraces the language of sexuality to express his love for Shams-e Tabrizi as a metaphor for his love for the Divine and the spiritual experiences that this companionship inspired. This is not uncommon in the work of mystic poets. In some instances, Rumi's verses are full-bodied and intimate, as the lover addresses his beloved Shams-e Tabrizi.

> You filled me with desire, gave me a taste.
> When you drew near, I smiled at your embrace.
> A beggar, I gave thanks to be so base.
> My master, you gave me your noble grace![25]

And:

> The price of love is peace and calm! Tempted,
> we fell. We died. He cared for me, he gave
> me drink, he ravaged me, he cherished me.[26]

Rumi is willing to discuss every private moment that passes between the lover and the beloved in his attempt to embody his longing for spiritual union. He shows us the first glance of lustful desire as he tries to escape from heavenly maidens.

> I turned to flee, but then they followed me.
> For fear of God, I will not say: That glance
> of sin created me, created me![27]

He writes of urgent, burning longing.

> The days have kept our bodies far apart,
> I swear by God, my heart is still with you.
> My heart is tender when my love is new,

sad and grieving when lovers then must part.
My heart sends you my messages of love—
no end. But I'm still thirsty! What to do?[28]

He even tells us of the despair of the abandoned lover, after the affair
is over.

He's gone! Calamity has seduced me.
You know how sad the one seduced will be.[29]

Rumi lived in the world of medieval Islam. His society freely
accepted a premodern understanding of sexuality and desire that
differs from our own. Rumi far predates modern notions of ho-
mosexuality and heterosexuality. Arab culture has always tolerated
same-gender friendship and intimacy within the boundaries of its
cultural norms, much more than conservative Western cultures do.
The sexuality of centuries past was less compartmentalized, less dif-
ferentiated, less medicalized than it is in our own time. To a certain
extent, same-sex love is suggested by every expression of devotion
to God where God is conceived of as male and the devotee is a man.
There are famous examples of this in Christian mystical poetry as
well. John Donne comes immediately to mind with his "Holy Sonnet
XIV," addressed to God.

• xv

Take me to you, imprison me, for I,
Except you enthrall me, never shall be free,
Nor ever chaste, except you ravish me.[30]

So, we are not in wholly unfamiliar territory when we read Rumi's
expressions of homoerotic desire. Yet, when such verses are ad-
dressed explicitly to Shams-e Tabrizi, the reader may become a little
apprehensive.

Franklin Lewis has argued that the norms of masculinity of Ru-
mi's time would have precluded any sexual relationship with Shams.[31]
Although many of Rumi's poems clearly express homoerotic themes,
these should be understood alongside the other tropes and metaphors

used in the poems—death, madness, drunkenness—as attempts to capture a spiritual ecstasy that is beyond description. At a distance of eight centuries, it is of course impossible to determine with any certainty precisely what level of physical intimacy Rumi and Shams shared. We can say for certain, however, that at whichever level his poems are understood, Rumi intends to point us in the direction of a love of the Divine Spirit that is ultimately transcendent and beyond any physical experience. On this quest, nothing is taboo. He will use any means to get us there through poetry and rhyme, including an idealized expression of homoerotic desire.

Wine and Death

Two other metaphors commonly found in Rumi's poems should be mentioned: wine and death. Rumi's poetry, as with much great poetry, is thoroughly transgressive.[32] Wine is strictly forbidden in Islam, but he exalts wine as the elixir of life and the only means of salvation.

> Come on! Come on! Come on, now! Let's be pure.
> Let's end our flirtation with temptation,
> let your glance cleanse us of degradation,
> return to the pure wine we drank when we
> sat in congregation, the cups passed 'round
> and offered up with no hesitation,
> pure, cool, shimmering nectar of salvation.[33]

Wine signifies intoxication with the spirit, separation from the material world, the drunkenness of love, the companionship of comrades, and ecstasy in the presence of the beloved.[34] Death implies unification with the beloved, and illicit sexual desire suggests yearning for spiritual union. The reader should enjoy the metaphors while remaining alert to their layered meanings.

Still, it is clear that no one can hope to achieve the goal of salvation, according to Rumi, without transgressing the perceived conventional boundaries of traditional Islamic practice.

The maidens in your court—so shy. They made
sweet love. They stole our hearts; we did the same.
We felt desire. Our friends warned us to be
afraid of love. We heard, but felt no shame.[35]

This is a wide and liberal interpretation of devotion to the Divine, based on an esoteric interpretation of the Qur'an, that is understood and praised by some (especially Sufi) Muslims. But it is interpreted by others as deviation from true Islam, and by a few as heresy.[36] Aware of this, Rumi writes:

Now reason shouts at me: "No! Don't step off
the righteous path or it will be your grave!"
But isn't death the only thing I crave?[37]

Again, death is a common theme in the Arabic poems. In death, Rumi finds reunion with Shams, extinction of the old self, and rebirth in the spirit. The old self must die, so that a new self can be born.

My Lord! My Savior! Full moon through night's dark!
You, Spirit of God and Spirit of love!
Lift the veils, my generous Patriarch!
With perfect justice, you slay your lovers,
cut down a mighty hero with your sword.
A glance of your love and he recovers,
masters become slaves of love, at your word.[38]

Love as Salvation

Rumi's poems point the way to salvation through the practice of love and imagination. This is clearly found in his Arabic poems. Although Sufi masters had taught the lessons of imagination and love long before Rumi,[39] he built on these traditions and encapsulated his mystic ecstasies in poems that enchant our spirits. For Rumi, through imagining (or recalling) his spiritual encounters with his beloved Shams, all separation vanishes in the union of love. The lover and the object of his love are one. This is the ultimate expression of union, and it applies to the Divine as much as to another human being. In their unity, they find salvation.

Rumi draws these insights from his interpretation of Islam. He finds in Islam a monism (or more accurately, a kind of nondualism) that allows no separation between a transcendent God and the manifestation of God's love in every aspect of creation, in all forms of beauty, and in every man and woman. There is only one true reality. Moreover, this reality can be understood to be either the Divine Essence—God, Allah, etc., who is infinite, unknowable, and utterly beyond human comprehension—or the manifestations of that essence in the world of creation, ultimately embodied in human form. It is the latter aspect of the Divine that Rumi approaches in his poems. Shams-e Tabrizi becomes the numinous. Rumi finds his salvation in utter devotion to Shams, whom he loves as his Savior and Messiah.

For Rumi, there is no access to God except through this intoxication of love. He rejects the criticism that he has thereby made Shams an idol. There is a traditional Islamic story that tells of the early conversion of a pagan tribesman of Arabia, who later became a renowned Muslim scholar.[40] He abandoned his old beliefs and accepted Islam when he saw a fox urinating on his idol as he approached it to offer prayers. Realizing that the idol was unable to protect itself from such an insult, he accepted Allah as the only true God. Accused by one of his contemporary scholars of another form of idolatry in his admiration of Shams, Rumi writes:

> Can I repent the sin of love this true?
> He says you're an idol that I worship,
> can't see the fox piss on my graven god.
> Nasir al-Din![41] He's the king of virtues!
> No foxes, only rabbits piss on love.[42]

All other considerations are set aside in the presence of love. Love is no idol; it is the true and only form of worship. Reason is cast aside, and no learning is required. The worshipper is saved by his own devotion and desire.

> If you're in love, join the congregation!
> If you still have a mind, then stay away.
> If you're pressed at home and parched by fire,
> I'll take you to a secret stream I know.
> You can drink, satisfy your desire—
> and, if your eyes can't see what's hidden there,
> just bring your thirst to serve our Messiah.[43]

Rumi offers an interpretation of Islam that knows nothing but love. It is the eternal faith of God. As in all faiths, the ultimate reality is one and indivisible. The purpose of faith is to unite all human beings in their quest for the Beloved. In one of his Persian quatrains, Rumi declares:

> On the seeker's path, wise men/fools are one.
> In his love, brothers and strangers are one.
> Go on! Drink the wine of the Beloved!
> In that faith, Muslims and pagans are one.[44]

The Struggle of Translation

Love Is My Savior is an attempt to translate into English a selection of Rumi's Arabic poems and verses in language that captures some of the power and excitement of the original texts. Rumi's Arabic poems, especially the long poems in the divan, are rarely translated or studied in English, with the exception of few translated by Franklin Lewis and other Rumi scholars.

In the Arab world, with its predominantly Sunni population, Rumi does not enjoy the same popularity as in the West. Arabs often become familiar with his work because of their interest in Sufism or through encounters with regions where he is famous like Iran, South Asia, and the West. Few Arab scholars have studied Rumi or published anything about his work.[45] The majority of those publications focus on his quatrains, translating them from Persian to Arabic or from an English translation of the Persian to Arabic.[46]

Love Is My Savior is the first English translation dedicated to Rumi's Arabic poems. We might think of these poems as Rumi's "well-kept secrets," now revealed to an English-speaking audience. They are as eloquent and powerful as his Persian verses, with a "sweetness, beauty, glory, and simplicity that are uniquely his—direct, fluid, rich, and void of pretense."[47]

The power of Rumi's verse has survived the test of centuries. The problem that confronts the translator is how to bring these verses into English in language that will retain that power. The selected Arabic poems in this book are highly compressed expressions of universal ideas written in the context of an ancient tradition of Arabic verse and Islamic culture. They refer to mystical themes, employ cultural tropes, and make references to Quranic verses that may be unfamiliar to most English readers. And, of course, Rumi lived some eight hundred years ago, which adds to the complexity of the task.

Yet the immense popularity today of Rumi's poetry in the West demonstrates that the centuries can be bridged. Dozens of translators and scores of volumes bring his Persian poetry into English in various styles and with more or less success. Occasionally, Rumi himself gets lost in the shuffle. The challenge for any translation of poetry is to bring a poem from one language and culture into another while remaining true to both the spirit and the meaning of the original. In this effort, a word-for-word translation is no help at all, and this book makes no attempt at that. Moreover, a translation that provides only the meaning of a poem, while it may give a thorough understanding of what the poet said, translates nothing of the beauty or excitement of the original. It loses the poem altogether, replacing it with a dull explanation. The worst outcome of any translation would be to take a poem that sounds natural, urgent, and transcendent in its original language and render it into English prose or flaccid poetry that is dull, ponderous, and awkward. While this might serve some scholarly purpose, it fails to capture the spirit of the poems. Freer translations have sometimes lost the specific context of Rumi's time and place, leaving us with a modern rendition of bland, New Age spirituality that was far from Rumi's context and intent.

The goal of this translation of Arabic verses was to craft translations in English that are successful as poems on their own terms, while remaining as close and true to the form and meaning of the originals as possible. When possible, the poems are translated line for line, so the Arabic reader can follow in the original language on the facing page. Rhyme and meter are such vital aspects of Rumi's poetry—of all classical poetry—that the translators felt that both had to be acknowledged. However, Arabic scanning has been, in most cases, exchanged for iambic pentameter, a familiar English convention. While it is foreign to Arabic poetry, this scheme gives the poems a rhythm that is comfortable to the English reader. English has very few opportunities for rhyme compared to Arabic, yet every effort was made to include rhyme prominently in the English versions. Rumi's verse in this collection is part of a large volume of his work where poems are always untitled. The titles used in this volume have been added by the translators, another English convention.

All this said, how is translation possible—especially the translation of poems? At first glance, any attempt to translate a poem from one language to another would seem futile. Every poem is a condensed form of language that captures the essence of human experience, which must appeal to the mind as much as to the heart, in images and words with deep cultural value, on multiple levels, suggesting multiple meanings. Even altering a poem in its original language by changing a few words here and there destroys the beauty of the work. How then can all the words of a poem be changed to a different language and preserve anything of the original meaning and effect?

However, poetry is not words. It is the language that we turn to when words fail to express our thoughts and feelings adequately. Poetry is, in fact, the attempt to move beyond words, to communicate states of mind and spirit that cannot be captured by language but which nonetheless must be expressed. The poem only points or suggests. It does not describe. It must conjure emotion in the reader. If it doesn't, then the poem is a failure. By some miracle of language, it is possible to find those emotions—across different languages and cultures, and across time—and to translate poems that will move new readers, but not by translating words. The translators must struggle to find the concepts, the music, and the images in a new language that can be crafted to the same effect as those in the original poem.

Poetry as Poetry

Love Is My Savior is a collaboration between an Arabic scholar, Nesreen Akhtarkhavari, and a poet, Anthony A. Lee, who knows no Arabic at all. The method of translation was simple. Akhtarkhavari created a literal translation of each line, preserving the original line structure. Then Lee took those lines and rewrote them to ensure the construction of acceptable poems in English. The first drafts were then returned to Akhtarkhavari for comment and correction, and then, back and forth, until both were satisfied with the results. The act of "translating" is accomplished through this process. The intent of the Arabic must be understood by the poet who seeks to find words and images in English that will be as clear and as powerful as those in the original. The gist of the poems and their cultural and historical contexts must be transferred by the Arabic scholar, while the clarity and structure of the English poem is ensured by the poet.

The quality of the resulting translation will depend upon the knowledge of the Arabic scholar and the skill of the English poet. This method is relatively uncommon in academia, which has traditionally relied on the unassisted language scholar to provide all translations of poetic texts. However, the necessity of collaboration has come to be appreciated recently.

Rumi's poems also present a serious challenge to the native Arabic speaker because they are written in medieval Arabic and call on the classical conventions of the Arabic poetic tradition. Quranic references must be identified and their relevance made clear. The meanings of archaic words and unfamiliar allusions must be found, deciphered, interpreted, and retold. Following all that, the poet must try to express the poem in a new language, with respect for the original, but in words and images that resonate in an alien culture. The translations should be startling, seductive, natural-sounding, and fascinating. They must call up a poetic world of their own, the mystic world of Rumi.

That is the point, of course. These poems must be approached and read as poems, not as works of philosophy, even in translation. Each poem invites us to enter a world that is unique and beyond time and space. We should find ourselves in another dimension where time stands still, we forget where we are sitting, and we are transfixed by the beauty of Rumi's mystical experiences, understood on no other terms but their own. We hope that these English translations will accomplish that goal for their readers as intensely, and indeed as ecstatically, as the original Arabic poems do for theirs.

NOTES

1. Love has been a common theme in Arabic literature since pre-Islamic times, and poetry has been the vehicle to express this—from the chaste and virgin love found in the poems of Ibn Hazm to the erotic and even the explicit, as in what is called unveiled literature (*al-adab al-makshouf*).

2. "Banner of Love."

3. For controversies concerning Rumi's date of birth, see Franklin D. Lewis, *Rumi: Past and Present, East and West; The Life, Teachings, and Poetry of Jalâl al-Din Rumi* (Oxford: Oneworld, 2007), 317–19. Unless otherwise noted, the account of Rumi's life relies on Lewis's biographical information. See especially, Lewis, *Rumi*, 9–37.

4. Shams al-Din Muhammad bin Ali Malekdad al-Tabrizi (1185–1248) was a Persian Sufi and poet.

5. In an unpublished essay, A. G. Ravan Farhadi suggests that Shams was a Sunni Shafi' scholar and followed the Prophet's teaching and practice. In contrast, some Sufis believe that Shams received his inspiration directly from God, as they believe they do.

6. Shams was a poor, wandering dervish, about sixty years old, and Rumi was a thirty-seven-year-old wealthy, distinguished scholar with a school and many disciples.

7. For a more detailed account of Rumi's life, see Lewis, *Rumi*.

8. See Lewis, *Rumi*, 184.

9. Most contemporary scholars agree that the legend of Shams's death at the hands of Rumi's students is unlikely (see Lewis, *Rumi*, 197–200).

10. See Annemarie Schimmel, *The Triumphal Sun: A Study of the Works of Jalaloddin Rumi* (New York: State University of New York Press, 1993).

11. See Lewis, *Rumi*, 193–99.

12. See Lewis, *Rumi*, 215–18.

13. "Speak Persian, though Arabic is sweeter: love indeed hath a hundred other tongues." *Masnavi*, Book 3, v. 3842, in *The Mathnawí of Jalálúddin Rumí*, ed. and trans. Reynold A. Nicholson (Tehran: So'ad Publisher, 2002), 427.

14. Abu al-Majd Majdud ibn Adam (1108–31/41), better known as Sanai, lived in Ghazna, was a Persian poet, and was the author of the first mystical poem in the Persian language. His work had great influence on Persian and Muslim literature. His best-known work is *The Garden of Truth and the Law of the Path*.

15. Abu Hamid bin Abu Bakr Ibrahim, better known as Farid ud-Din Attar, was a Persian poet and theoretician of Sufism from Nishapur in Iran. See the excellent translation of his work by Afkham Darbandi and Dick Davis, *The Conference of the Birds* (New York: Penguin Books, 1984).

16. Sayed Burhan al-Din Muhaqqiq Turmudi, Rumi's first teacher after his father, was a lover of Sanai and his work, which he frequently shared with Rumi and others.

17. Afzal Iqbal, in *The Life and Work of Jalauddin Rumi* (London: Oxford University Press, 1999), suggests that Rumi was greatly influenced by Attar and tried to imitate him. Frank Lewis and others confirm that Rumi met Attar during his early travels, and Attar was impressed by him, and gave him a copy of his divan *The Conference of the Birds*.

18. Abdu'l Mughit Husayn al-Hallaji, known as Mansour Al-Halaj, was a controversial Arabic-speaking Persian mystic poet whose execution for his beliefs is considered a major turning-point in the history of Islamic mysticism.

19. Abu Abd Allah Muhammad ibn Ali ibn Muhammad ibn al-Arabi was a Berber Andalusian Sufi mystic and philosopher.

20. Franklin Lewis suggests that Rumi became acquainted with Arabic poetry, especially the work of al-Mutanabi, at an early age and improved his knowledge when he was student in Syria (Lewis, *Rumi*, 315).

21. Jalal al-Din Rumi, *Kulliyat Shams ya Divan-e Kabir*, vols. 1 and 2, ed. Badi-u-Zaman Furuzanfar (Tehran: Amir Kabir Press, 1957). An unpublished collection of the Arabic poems by A. G. Ravan Farhadi was also consulted.

22. In his book, *Rumi and Islam: Selections from His Stories, Poems, and Discourses* (Woodstock, VT: SkyLight Paths Publishing, 2004), Ibrahim Gamard, an American Sufi teacher and scholar, illustrates this argument with numerous examples drawn from Rumi's work that specifically reference Islamic texts and traditions. This is further demonstrated in the annotated translation *The Quatrains of Rumi: Ruba 'iyat- i Jalaluddin Muhammad Balkhi-Rumi* (San Rafael, CA: Sophia Perennis, 2008), translated by A. G. Ravan Farhadi in collaboration with Ibrahim Gamard, where references to Islamic concepts are noted.

23. "The Cupbearer Will Explain."

24. There are minor breaks in some of the poems' scales and rhymes in both Rumi's Persian and Arabic poems. This is to be expected since his poems were supposedly recorded by his scribe as Rumi spontaneously recited them, with no opportunity to go back and edit them.

25. "A Dream."

26. "The Price of Love."

27. "I Fell in Love with Angels."

28. "I Climbed to Heaven."

29. "It Was a Celebration!"

30. John Donne, *John Donne Poems*, ed. Sir Herbert Grierson, The Franklin Library edition (Oxford University Press, 1933), 359. Modern spellings used here.

31. Lewis, *Rumi*, 320–23.

32. For a detailed discussion of imagery in Rumi's poetry, see Schimmel, *The Triumphal Sun*.

33. "Let's Be Pure."

34. See Lewis, *Rumi*, 324–26.

35. "You Sang of Love, So We Came."

36. Many contemporary Sunni scholars find Rumi's poems unacceptable. Some condemn his teachings and warn their followers against reading his work. Other Muslim scholars see him a religious leader, a brilliant thinker, and a saint.

37. "Love Is My Savior."

38. "Light of My Soul."

39. For example, this can be found in the poetry of Sanai and Attar.

40. Abu Dhar al-Ghifari al-Kinani, also known as Jundub ibn Junadah ibn Sufian, was one of the earliest to convert to Islam and a renowned Muslim scholar.

41. This is a possible reference to Nasir ud-Din al-Tousi, a Muslim scholar and contemporary of Rumi who aided the Mongol defeat of the Ismaili Nizari and the conquest of Alamut Castle by the Mongols in 1256 CE The Ismailis believe that Shams, and even Rumi, were affiliated with their sect.

42. "I Climbed to Heaven."

43. "Your Wine Lights the World."

44. Amin Banani and Anthony A. Lee, trans., *Rumi: 53 Secrets from the Tavern of Love: Poems from the Rubiayat of Mevlana Rumi* (Ashland, OR: White Cloud Press, 2014), 3.

45. See Lewis, *Rumi*, 553.

46. Ibrahim al-Dosoughi Shata translated the complete *Masnavi* into Arabic. al-Dosoughi Shata was an Egyptian writer and scholar of Persian literature (1943–98) who taught at the University of Cairo and translated a number of Persian works, including Rumi's *Masnavi* into Arabic. Eissa Ali al-Akoub translated Rumi's discussions in *Kitab Feeh Ma Feeh Ahadeth Mawlana Jalal Al-Din Al-Rumi Sha'ir Al-Sufia Al-Akbar*, published by Dar Al-Fikr (2002). The first compilation dedicated to Rumi's Arabic poems was published in 2011 by Al-Majma al-Adabi al-Tunisi in *Al-Diwn al-Arabi li-Maulana Jallal al-Din al-Rumi*, (Tunis, 2011).

47. Aref al-Zaghloul et. al, trans., *Mukhtarat min a-She'ar al-Farisi*. (Muasasat Abdul Aziz Saud Babteen: Iran, Tehran, 2000), 88.

Love
IS MY SAVIOR

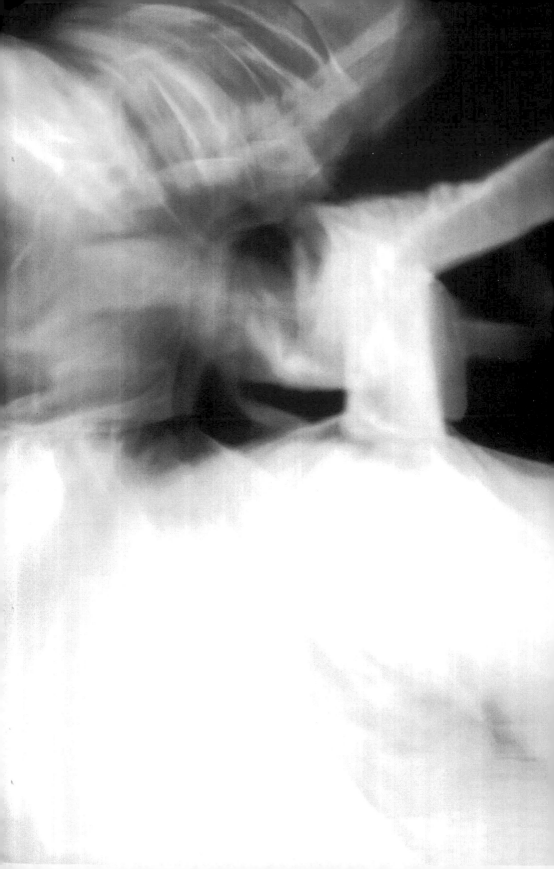

Leave Behind Temptation

دع عنك إغواءنا

تعالو بنا نصفو

تَعالوا بِنا نَصفو نُخَلّي التَدلُلا
وَمِن لَحظكُم نُجلي الفؤَادَ مِن الجلا
نَعودُ إلى صَفوِ الرَحيقِ بِمَجلسٍ
تَدورُ بِنا الكاساتُ تَتلو على الوَلا
رَحيقاً رَقيقاً صافياً مُتلألِئاً
فَنَخلوا بِها يَوماً ويَوماً على المَلا
شرَاباً إذا ما يَنشرُ الريحُ طِيبَها
تَحنُّ إليها الوحشُ مِن جانبِ الفَلا
خَوابي الحُميّرة اِفتَحوها لِعشرةٍ
بِمفتاح لُقياكُم لِيرخصِ ما غَلا
يُتابعُ سُكرُ الراح سُكرَ لِقائكُم
فَيسكرُ مَن يَهوى ويَفنى مَن قَلا
أُناشدكُم بِالله تَعفونَ إنني
لَقد ذُبتُ بِالأشواقِ والحبِ والوَلا
لمولّا ترى في حُسنِهِ وجمالِهِ
أماناً مِن الآفاتِ والموتِ والبَلا
سَقى الله أرضاً شَمسَ دينٍ يَدوسُها
كَلا الله تَبريزاً بأحسنِ ما كَلا.

Let's Be Pure

Come on! Come on! Come on, now! Let's be pure.
Let's end our flirtation with temptation,
let your glance cleanse us of degradation,
return to the pure wine we drank when we
sat in congregation, the cups passed 'round
and offered up with no hesitation,
pure, cool, shimmering nectar of salvation.
We drank in secret—some days in the street.
Our wine's perfume was carried off so far
even the desert beasts yearned for its sweet.
But you're the key that opens up the jars
of that red flow, when friends sit at your feet.
There, every priceless thing becomes a lie.
There, drunk on wine and drunk on you, I lie.
I love and drink, and when I hate I die.
My friends, forgive me! My Lord, hear my cry!
I'm melting with desire and love's duty
for my Master—Just look at his beauty!—
my refuge from death and calamity.
May God bless any land where Shams may be!
God gave Tabriz the best of his bounty.

ابشروا بصمت

اَبشِروا يَا قَومُ هَذا فَتحُ بَاب
قَد نَجوتُم مِن شِتاتِ الاغتِراب
اِفرَحوا قَد جاءَ مِيقاتُ الرِضا
مِن حَبيبٍ عِندهُ أمُّ الكِتاب"
قَالَ "لا تَأَسوا عَلى مَا فَاتَكُم"
اِذ بَدى بَدرُ خَروقٌ للحِجاب"
ذا مُناخٌ اَوقِفوا بُعراننَا
ذا نَعيمٌ لَيسَ يُحصيهِ الحِساب
إنَّ فِي عَتبِ الهَوا اَلفَ الوَفا
أنَّ فِي صَمتِ الوَلا لُطفُ الخِطاب
قَد سَكتنا فَافهَموا سِرَ السُكُوت
يَا كِرامُ الله اَعلَم بِالصَّواب.

4 •

Rejoice in Silence

People, rejoice! His gate is open wide.
We are not alone—we're saved at his side.
People, rejoice! This is the day of grace!
Your lover holds the Holy Book in place.
Don't fret about the things that you have lost.*
The full Moon rose! It scattered all that dross.
Camp here! Tie your camel at this station.
This is heaven past all calculation.
In love's shame, there is a secret silence,
the silence of fidelity. No words.
Be silent! Know the secret of silence.
Be patient! God guards his truth in silence.

---

*This is a quote from Quran 57:23.

لواء العشق

يَا مَن لِواءُ عِشقكَ لا زالَ عَالياً
قَد خابَ مَن يكونُ مِن العِشقِ خالياً

نادى نسيمُ عِشقِكَ في أنفس الوَرى
أحياكُم جَلالي، جَلَ جَلاليا

الحبُ والغرامُ، أصولُ حَياتِكُم
قَد خابَ مَن يَظلُ مِن الحُبِ سالياً

في وجنةِ المُحبِ، سُطورُ رَقيمَةٌ
طُوبى لمن يَصيرُ لمعناهُ تالياً

يَا عابساً تفرَّقَ في الهَمِ حَالهُ
باللهِ تَستمِع لمقالي وَحاليا

يَا مَن أذلَّ عقلَكَ، نَفسُ الهَوى تَعي
مِن ذُلّةِ النُفوسِ سَريعاً مَعالياً

يَا مُهملًا معيشته فِي مَحبةٍ
أُسكتْ. كَفى الإله مُعيناً وكالياً.

Banner of Love

You, who still wave the banner of love high!
if you're not in love, you have missed your goal.
He calls! The breeze of love must find your soul.
Glory resurrected you, glory made you whole!
If you're not in love, life has passed you by.
The foundation of life is love's sweet cry.
On the face of the Beloved holy
verses lie. Blessed be he who will read them.
Destroyed by troubles, how you grieve and sigh . . .
By God! Listen to my proclamation!
He knows who caused your mind's devastation.
From abasement, your soul will always rise.
You've abandoned all for love's enterprise.
Be still. God is your helper. He's the prize.

عشِقت مِلاحا

أنَا لا أقسِمُ إلا بِرجالٍ صَدقونا
أنَا لا أعشقُ إلا بِمِلاحٍ عَشِقونا
فَصَبوا ثُمَّ صَبِينا، فأتَوا ثُمَّ أتَينا
لَهمُ الفضلُ عَلينا، لِمَ؟ مَمّا سَبقُونا
فَفتَّحنا حَدقاتٍ وغَنِمنا صَدقاتٍ
وسَرقنا سَرقاتٍ، فإذا هُم سَرقُونا
فظَفَرنا بِقلوبٍ وعَلِمنا بِغيوبٍ
فَسقى اللهُ وَسُقيا لِعُيونٍ رَمَقُونا
لَحِقَ الفضلُ وإلا لَهُتِكنا وهَلَكنا
فَفَررنا ونَفَرنا، فإذا هُم لَحِقونا
أنا لَولاي أُحاذِرُ سَخَط اللهِ لقلتُ:
"رَمَقَ العينِ لِزاما خَلقونا خَلقونا"
فَتَعرّضَ لِشموسٍ، مُكِّنت تَحتَ نُفوسٍ
وسَقونا بِكؤوسٍ رَزقونا، رَزقونا.

I Fell in Love with Angels

Now, I swear by those men who do not lie.
I fell in love with angels, and they with me.
They were mad with love, and so was I.
After that, I came, and they came with me.
I woke up. I took hold of God's bounty.
I took from them before they took from me.
I looked in my heart, learned God's mystery.
Blessed! Blessed be! those eyes that looked at me.
I would have died, but He sent His mercy.
I turned to flee, but then they followed me.
For fear of God, I will not say: That glance
of sin created me, created me!
Don't flee! Find Shams inside your soul, instead.
He pours out wine, gives us our daily bread.

سبا قلبي

أخي! أرأيتَ جمالًا سَبا القلوبَ سَبا؟
وهَل أتاكَ حديثٌ جَلا العُقولَ جَلا؟
ألستَ مَن يَتمنَّى الخُلودَ في طَربٍ؟
ألا انتبه وتَيقظ، فقد أتاكَ أتى
يُقرُّ عَينَكَ بدرٌ وفي جَبينَتِهِ
سَعادةُ ومَرامٌ وعزةُ وسَنا
وسَكرَةُ لفؤادي مِن شَمائِلِهِ
كأنّها مَلأت كأسَنا وأسقانا
عَجائبٌ ظَهَرَت بَين صَفو غُرّتِهِ
تلألأت لَسَناهُ بِمهجتي وصَفا.

He Stole My Heart!

Brother! See the Beauty who stole my heart! Stole it!
And don't you hear the voice that cleaned my soul? Cleaned it!
Aren't you the one looking for immortality
in music? Look up! He comes to you now. He comes!
See! The full Moon! Let your eyes drink their fill. Their fill!
I'm happy, just staring here, drunk on his beauty.
On his brow he brings us love, pride, and light. And light!
As if he filled my cup and gave me wine. Pure wine!
As if the brilliance of his face makes miracles.
His light flashed in my heart. I am made pure. Made pure!

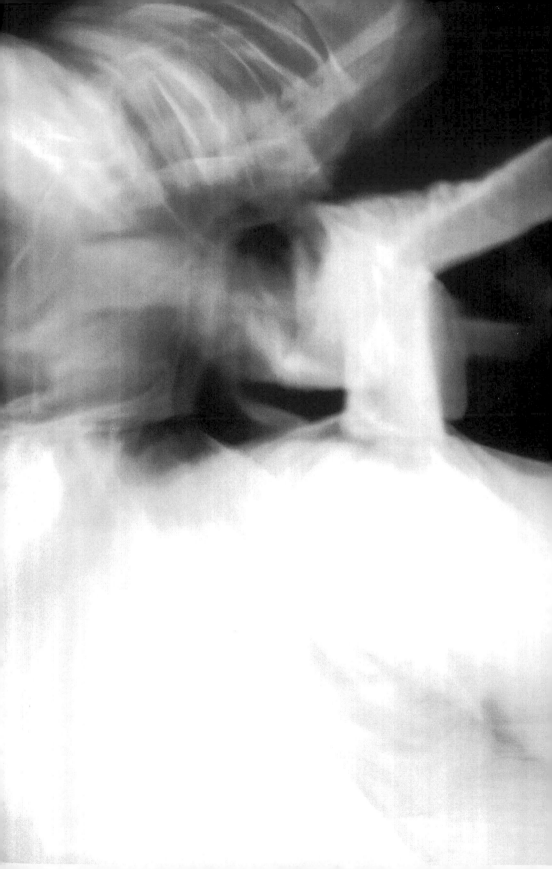

You Sang of Love

غنيّت للحب

حدا الحادي بحب فأتينا

حَدا الحَادي صَبَاحاً بِهَواكُم فَأَتينا
صَدَّنا عَنكُم ظِباءُ حَسدونا فَأَبينا
وَتَلاقينا مِلاحاً في فِناكُم خَفِراتٍ
فَتعاشقنا بِغُنجٍ، فَسبونا، وسَبينا
عَذَلَ العاذِلُ يومًا عَن هَواكُم نَاصِحيا
أن يَخافوا عَن هَواكُم، فَسَمِعنا وعَصينا
ورَأيناكُم بُدوراً في سَمواتِ المَعالي
فَاستَتَرنا كَنُجومٍ بِهَواكُم واهتدينا
بَدرُنا مِثلَ خَطيبٍ، أَمَّنَا في يَوم عِيدِ
فَاصطَفَينا حَولَ بَدرٍ في صَلوةٍ اقتَدينا
فَدَهِشنا مِن جَمالِ يوسفٍ، ثُمَّ أَفقنا
فإذا كاساتُ راحٍ، كدماءٍ بِيدينا
فَبلا فَم شَربِنا وَبِلا روحٍ سَكِرنا
وَبِلا رَأسٍ فَخِرنا وبِلا رِجلٍ سَرينا
فبلا أنفٍ شَممنا وَبِلا عَقلٍ فَهِمنا
وَبِلا شِدقٍ ضَحِكنا وَبِلا عَينٍ بَكينا
نورُ اللهُ زَماناً، حَازَنا الوَصلُ أماناً
وَسَقا اللهُ مَكاناً بِحبيب التَقَينا
وشَربِنا مِن مَدامٍ سَكِرٍ ذاتُ قُوامٍ
في قُعودٍ وقِيامٍ فَظَهرنا وَاختَفَينا
فَهَزِزنا غُصنَ مَجدٍ، فَنَثَرنا ثَمرَ وُجدٍ
فِإذا نَحنُ سُكارى فَطَفِقنا وَاجتَبينا

You Sang of Love, So We Came

This morning, you sang of love, so we came.
Jealous, wild bucks blocked our way. But we came.
The maidens in your court—so shy. They made
sweet love. They stole our hearts; we did the same.
We felt desire. Our friends warned us to be
afraid of love. We heard, but felt no shame.
Like stars, we saw your full moon in the sky,
then hid ourselves behind your light. We came.
Moon! Our guide! On that Holy Day you said
the prayer. In lines behind, we did the same.
Stunned by the beauty of Joseph, I woke.
My hands were full—blood-red wine in two cups.
Without a mouth, I drank. With no soul,
I found bliss. With no head, I was proud. No feet,
I walked. Without a nose, I smelled perfume.
With no mind—suddenly—I understood.
Then, with no mouth, I laughed. No eyes, I cried.
God bless the place I found my beloved!
when he lit the flash of our reunion,
where he watered that garden, as we watched,
finding peace and joy in our communion,
where we stood, then sat—gulped strong wine till we
disappeared. We came back all confusion.
That day, we pulled down a branch of glory,
spilled seeds of love—ecstasy's diffusion.
We got so drunk, we won a victory!
We found ourselves here among God's chosen.

ثمن العشق

سَبقَ الجدُّ إلينا نَزلَ الحُبُ عَلينا
سَكنَ العِشقُ لَدينا، فَسكنا وَثوينا
زمنُ الصَحو نَدامة، زَمنُ السُكرِ كَرامة
خطرُ العِشقِ سَلامة، فَفُتنا وفُنينا
فَسَقانا، وسَبانا، وكَلانا ورَعانا
ومِن الغيبِ أتانا، فَدَعانا وأتينا
فَوجدناهُ رَفيقاً، وَمَناصاً وَطَريقاً
وَشَراباً، وَرَحيقاً، فَسَقانا وَسَقينا
صَدقَ العِشقُ مَقالاً، كَرُمَ الحُبُ تَوالى
ومِنَ الخَلفِ تَعالى، فَوفانا وَوَفينا
مَلاءَ الطارقُ كاساً، طَردَ الكَأسُ نُعاساً
مَهدَ السُكرُ أساساً وعلى ذاكَ بَنينا
فَرأينا خَافرات ومَغانٍ حَسنات
سُرُجاً في ظلمات، فَدُهشنا وهَوينا
فاليهُنَّ نَظرَنا، فَشَكرنا وسَكِرنا
ومِنَ السُكرِ عَبرنا، كَفتِ العِبرةُ زَينا
فَرجعنا بِيسارٍ، ورُبى ذَاتَ قَرارٍ
وحَكينا لِمشاةٍ وشَهِدنا والَينا

The Price of Love

The Truth walked in, and love fell all around.
Love found us. We died. So, we settled down.
Drunk and so full of pride! Shamed when sober!
The price of love is peace and calm! Tempted,
we fell. We died. He cared for me, he gave
me drink, he ravaged me, he cherished me.
He came from nowhere. He called me. I came.
Lover! Savior! My Path! My Elixir!
You gave me a cup. I passed it around.
What you said was true: love's blessings astound.
From behind, you rose, you filled me. I'm bound.
He knocked, poured a cup. I woke up! We built
intoxication as our foundation.
We saw shy women. Such fascination!
Lanterns in the dark. Stunned adoration!
We stared, grateful. Pure intoxication!
Still drunk, we carried on, found our reward.
We returned with wealth, with culture, and adorned
with elation. To every passerby,
we confessed our blessed revelation.

ساقي الروح

يَا مُخجِلَ البَدرِ اشرِقنا بِلأ لاءِ
يَا سَاقِيَ الرُوحِ اَسكِرنا بِصهباءِ
لا تَبخلَنَّ وأوفِر راحَنا مَدَداً
حَتى تُنادِمَ في أَخذٍ واعطاءِ
دَعنا يُنافِس فِي الصهباءِ مِن سَكَرٍ
بِالسُكرِ يَذهلُ مِن وَصفٍ واسماءِ
خَوابِي الغَيبِ قَد أملأَتُها مَدداً
رَاحاً يُطَهِّرُ مِن شُحٍ وشَحناءِ.

Drunken Brothers

You! who make the full moon stand ashamed,
come here and shine your brightest light on me.
You! who pour out nectar for the soul.
Come here! Make me as drunk as drunk can be.
Don't stop! More! Give me all the wine I claim,
till you and I two drunken brothers be,
back and forth, vying over ecstasy.
Now, I'm so drunk I can't recall your name
or find your face. I'm filled with mystery,
wine that saves me from spite and misery.

هذه العين

بَكت عَيني غَداةَ البَين دَمعاً
وأُخرى بِالبُكا بَخِلت عَلينا
فَعاقبتُ التي بَخِلت عَلينا
بِأن غَمَّضتها يَومَ اِلتَقَينا.

This Eye

This eye shed tears when you left me again.
This eye stayed dry, held back its tears again.
So, I taught that dry miser a lesson.
I kept it shut when I saw you again.

عشق لا يُمل

أَفدي قَمَراً لاحَ عَلينا وَتَلأَلأَ
مَا أَحسَنَهُ رَبِّ تَبارك وتَعالى
قد حَلَ بِروحي فَتَضاعفتْ حَياةُ
واليومَ نَأى عَني عِزاً وجلالًا
أَدعوهُ سِراراً وانُاديهِ جِهاراً
أَن أَبِدلني الصَبوةَ طَيفاً وخَيالًا
لَو قَطَّعَني دَهري لا زلتُ أُنادي
كي تَختَرِقَ الحُجبُ ويُروينَ وصالًا
لا مَلَّ مِن العِشقِ لَو مَرَّ قُرونٌ
حاشاهُ مَلالًا بي حاشايَ مَلالًا
العَاشِقُ حوتٌ وَهَوى العِشقِ كَبحرٍ
هَل مَلَّ إذا ما سَكَنَ الحُوتُ زُلالًا؟

He's Never Bored with Love

Yes! My soul will be sacrificed for you!
You are the full moon. You rise, and you shine.
Praised and glorified be God for that shine!
You invaded my soul, doubled my life.
Then, you left—with that noble pride of thine.
Today, I pray to you in secret, or
I shout out loud these mad love dreams of mine.
Life tears me to pieces, and still I shout:
Pierce through these veils! Let me drink your love's wine!
Centuries of loving, and he's never
bored with love. Never will his love decline.
My lover is a whale, and my desire
pure water—an ocean—with no end time.
Can a whale grow bored in a pure ocean?

• 23

ماذا حدث؟

أبْصَرَت رُوحي مَليحاً زَلزَلَت زِلزالها
انعَطَش رُوحي فقُلتُ وَيحَ رُوحي مَالها
ذاقَ مِن شَعشاعِ خَمرِ العِشقِ رُوحي جُرعةً
طارَ في جَوِ الهَوى واستَقلَعت أثقالها
صارَ رُوحي في هَواهُ غارِقاً حَتى دَرى
لَو تَلقاه ضَريرٌ، تائهٌ أحوالها
فِي الهَوى مَن لَيسَ فِي الكَونين بَدرٌ مِثلُهُ
إنَّ رُوحي فِي الهَوى مِن لا تَرى أمثالها
لَم تَمِل رُوحي إلى مَالٍ إلى أن أعشَقت
رامتِ الأموالَ كَي تَنثُرَ لَهُ أموالها
لَم تَزل سُفنُ الهَوى تَجري بِها مُذ أصبَحَت
في بِحارِ العِزِ والاقبالِ يَوماً، يا لَها
عَينُ رُوحي قَد أصابتها فأرَدتها بِها
حِينَ عَدَّت فَضلَها واستكثَرَت أعَمالها
أفلَحت مِن بَعدِ هُلكٍ، إنَّ أعوانَ الهَوى
اعتَنوا فِي أمرِها، أن خَففوا أحمالها
آهُ رُوحي مِن هَوى صَدرٍ كَبيرٍ فائقٍ
كُلُّ مَدحٍ قَالَها فيهِ ازدَرَت أقوالها
يَيأسُ النَّفسُ اللِقاءَ مِن وِصالٍ فائتٍ
حين تَتلو فِي كِتابِ الغَيب مِن أفعالها
حَبذا احسانُ مَولىً عادَ رُوحاً إذ نَفث
ناولَتها شَربَةً، صَفَّى لَها أحوالها
إنَّ رُوحي تَقشَعُ اللقَياتِ في المَاضي مَداً
ثُمَّ لا تُبصِرُ مضى إذ تَفكَرُ استِقبالها
اختَفى العِشقُ الثَقيلُ في ضَميري دُرَّةً
إنَّ رُوحي اثقَلَت مِن دُرَّةٍ قَد شالها
مِثلُهُ إن اثقَلَ اليومُ المَخاضُ حُرَّةً
اوقَعَتها فِي رَدى لَم تُغنِها أحجالها
غَيرَ أنَّ سَيداً جادَت لَها الطاقَهُ
أن رُوحي رَبوةٌ وَاستَنزلَت اطلالها
سيداً مَولىً عَزيزاً كامِلاً في امرِه
شَمسُ دينٍ مَالِكٍ، اوفَت لَها آمالها

What Happened to Me?

He shook my core! My soul saw such beauty!
Thirst! Desire! I said: "What happened to me?"
I tasted the wine of love, you see.
And now free, I soared to love's horizon.
I left my burden there, drowning in love.
A blind man can look up and see my love.
No Moon like him in this world or the next.
There's nothing more than this. See: I'm in love.
I never wanted wealth, but now I'm hexed.
Now, I search for gold on any pretext
to shower him with riches, just for love.
The ship of love sails from eternity—
Praised be!—on the sea of his great glory.
With just a glance, my Soulmate murdered me
when I counted his virtues and blessings.
I lay dying. Maidens of love saved me—
saved my spirit—saved me from misery.
My soul! I love his mighty chest. Praise him!
—though every praise is but a mockery.
I have no hope of seeing him again.
His virtues, recited from the Secret
Tablet—Praise him!—restored my troubled soul.
I remember our union in times past.
So clear, I see no death when I see him.
Desire left me. It became a pearl.
My heart grows heavy as I wear that pearl,
as a princess in the pain of labor,
who dies in her travail—jewels won't save her!
But my Master showed me every kindness.
My soul, a fertile field, begs him to come.
Master, Beloved, perfect in all things!
Shams ud-Din, Master! Dreams of life he brings.

صادَفَ المَولى بِروحي وَهي فِي ذُلِّ الرَدى
مِن زَمانٍ أكرَمتهُ مَا رَأت إذلالَها
جَاءَ مِن تَبريزَ سِربالٌ نَسيجٌ بِالهوى
اكتَست رُوحي صَباحاً انزَعَت سِربالَها
قَالتِ الروحُ اِفتِخاراً اِصطَفانا فَضلُهُ
ثُمَّ غارَت بَعدَ حِينٍ مِن مَقالٍ نالَها.

My Master found me dead and in disgrace.
I honored him and rose from that bad place.
He came from Tabriz, wearing robes of love,
and I—just dressed in light—threw off my clothes.
My prideful soul cried: "He chose me alone!"
Then it collapsed, from those words that he loathes.

لا تظلمونا

يَا كَالِينا، يا حَاكِمِينا،
يَا مَالِكِينا، لا تَظلُمونا
يَا ذَا الفَضائِل، زَهرَ الشَمائِل
سَيفَ الدَّلائِلَ، لا تَظلُمونا
يا نِعمَ سَاقي، حُلو التَلاقي
مُرَّ الفِراقِ، لا تَظلُمونا
فِي القلبِ بَارق، مِثلَ الطَوارقِ
بَينَ المَشارِقِ، لا تَظلُمونا
نَادى المُنادي، فِي كُلِ وَادي
لا بِالعِنادِ، لا تَظلُمونا
أفديكَ رُوحي، عِندَ الصَّبُوحِ
يَا ذَا الفُتوح، لا تَظلُمونا
هَذا فُؤَادي، فِي العشقِ بَادي
فِي الحُبِ غادي، لا تَظلُمونا
اسمعْ كَلامي، نَومي حَرامي
عِندَ الكِرامِ، لا تَظلُمونا
عِشقي حِصاني، نَحو المَعاني
هَذا كَفاني، لا تَظلُمونا
العشقُ حَالٌ، مُلكُ ومَالٌ
نَومي مُحالٌ، لا تَظلُمونا

Have Mercy!

You who scourged me! You who commanded me!
You are my Master. Have mercy on me!
You're the flower of virtue; you're my saint,
my sword of proofs! Have mercy on me!
You pour the best of wines, sweet in union,
bitter in separation. Have mercy!
Your light is in my heart, the most brilliant
star of the stars in the East. Have mercy!
I cried out to you from every valley;
I cried out so patiently. Have mercy!
I am your sacrifice each dawn. You bring
me victory. Lord! Have mercy on me!
Here is my heart, raving mad and in love!
I wait for you at daybreak. Have mercy!
Listen! The holy ones are telling me
that I must not sleep. Have mercy on me!
Love is my protector—full of meaning—
and for me that is enough. Have mercy!
This love is a place of wealth and power
where sleep is impossible. Have mercy!

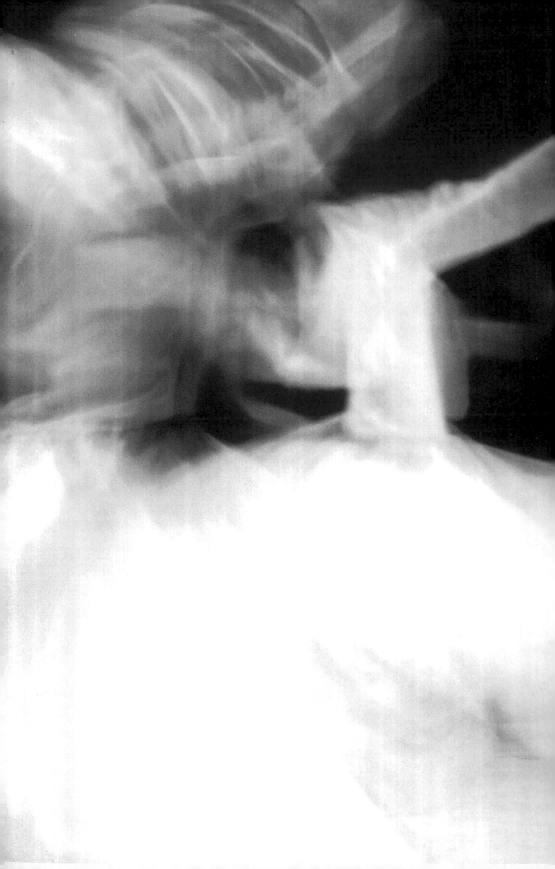

Come, Let's Pray

تعال نحتفل

كلنا سكارى

تَعالُوا كُلُّنا ذَا اليَومَ سَكرى
بِأَقداحٍ تُخامِرُنا وتَترى
سَقانا رَبُّنا "كَأساً دِهاقاً"
فَشُكراً ثُمَّ شُكراً ثُمَّ شُكراً
تَعالوا إنَّ هَذا يَومُ عِيدٍ
تَجَلّى فِيهِ مَا تَجرونَ جَهراً
طَوارِقُ زُرنَنا واللَيلُ سَاجي
فَما أَبقَينَ فِي التَضييقِ صَدراً
زِكَف هَر يِكي دَرياي بَخشِش* نَثَّرنَ جَواهِراً جَمّاً وَوفراً.

We're All Drunk

Come by our place today! We are all drunk.
Our cups are full of wine, and we're all drunk.
The cup God gave us, it's running over.
Give thanks, give thanks—thanks for this charity!
Come by our place. It's a celebration!
Our longing now made plain for all to see.
Our lovers came to us in the dark of night—
in our hearts they left no shame, no anxiety.
"Each held in open palms a generous sea,"*
and scattered jewels for us abundantly.

---

*This line is in Persian in the original poem.

تعال نصلي

يَا سَاقِيَ الُمدامةِ حَيٌّ عَلى الصَلا
إملأ زُجاجَنا بِحُميّا فَقد خَلا
جِسمي زُجاجَتي ومُحّياكَ قَهوتي
يَا كَامِلَ الَملاحةِ واللُطفِ والعُلا
مَا فَازَ عَاشِقٌ بِمُحَيّاكَ سَاعةً
إلا وفي الصُدودِ تَلاشى مِن البَلا
الَموتُ في لِقائِك يَا بَدرُ طَيبُ
حَاشاكَ بَل لِقاؤكَ أمنٌ مِن البَلا
لَّما تَلا هَواكَ صِفاتاً لُهجتي
فِيها حَمائُمُ يَتَلَقيّن مَا تَلا
اسقِني الُمدامةَ مِن طَرفِك البَهي
حَتى جَلا فُؤادي مِن أحسنِ الِجلا.

Come, Let's Pray!

You're offering me wine? So come, let's pray!
Come fill my cup with wine! It's dry today.
My body, the wine flask. Your face, my drink.
You're pure beauty, God's splendor on display!
Any lover who knows you for an hour
will die of longing when you go away.
Moon! My death in meeting you was sweet!
You're my high refuge from disaster's sway.
Whenever your love sang its melody,
the birds of my heart answered every note.
Your sacred trace is wine to drink for me.
My soul made pure and bright by your bounty.

زائر الليل

إِيهِ يَا اَهلَ الفَراديسِ اِقرأوا مَنشورَنا
وَادهِشوا مِن خَمرِنا واستَسمِعوا نَاقورنا
حُورِكُم تَصفَّر عِشقاً تَنحني مِن نارِه
لَو رَأت في جُنحِ لَيلٍ أَو نَهارٍ حُورَنا
جاءَ بَدرٌ كامِلٌ قَد كَدَّرَ الشَمسَ الضُحى
في قِيانٍ خَادِماتٍ وَاستقروا دُورَنا
اَلفُ بَدرٍ حَولَ بَدري، سُجَّداً خَرّوا لَهُ
طَيَبوا مَا حَولَنا واستَشرَقوا دَيجورَنا
قَد سَكِرنا مِن حَواشي بَدرِهِم، اَكرِم بِهم
اِستَجابوا بِغِنَا وَاستكثَروا مَيسورَنا.

Night Visitors

People of Paradise! This is my word!
Come, drink this wine. Let my trumpet be heard!
Holy virgins, glowing with love, bent to
my passion, found my light. Day and night blurred.
The moon rose at midday, eclipsed the sun.
At my door with brilliant maids, he entered.
He stayed. A thousand moons circled round him,
sweetened the earth, lit up my dark center.
I'm drunk on moonlight. She gave graciously,
filled my desires, and took my gifts with her.

الساقي يشرح

مَولانا، مَولانا، أغنانا، أغنانا
أمسينا عَطشانا، أصبحنا، رَيانا
لا تَأسى، لا تَنسى، لا تَخشى طُغيانا
أوطانا أوطانا، مِن أجلِكَ أوطانا
شَرِّفنا، آنِسنا، إن كُنتَ سَكرانا
يَا بارقُ، يَا طارق، عانِقنا عَريانا
مَن كانَ أرضياً، مَا جاءَ مَرضياً
فليعبُد فليعبُد، فُرقاناً فُرقانا
مَن كَانَ عِلوياً، قَد جاءَ حُلوياً
نُرويهِم مَعنانا الوانا الوانا
والباقي والباقي، بَينهُ يَا سَاقي
يا مُحسنُ يا مُحسن، إحساناً إحساناً.

The Cupbearer Will Explain

My rich Master! You gave me riches first,
then gave me drink when I was full of thirst.
My brothers! Don't despair! You won't be cursed.
Don't forget him! No fear of tyranny.
I found my home in his homeland. Come see!
So, honor me. Get drunk! Come here and be
my companion. Radiant seeker! Come
naked and embrace me. In earthly clothes
you can't be saved or blessed with ecstasy.
Then let pure being worship pure being.
The holy souls came here with faith—from cups
of many colors drank truth and clarity.
Let the cupbearer explain the rest!
He is kind. Let us drink his charity.

القمر الساطع

نَفسي بِهوى الحبيبِ فازَت
لَمّا رأت الكؤوس دارَت

مَدَت يَدها إلى رَحيقٍ
وَالنفسُ بِنورهِ استَنارَت

لَمّا شَرِبتهُ نَفَسٌ وِتراً
خَفَّت وَتَصاعَدت وَطارَت

لاقَت قَمراً إذا تَجلى
الشمسُ مِن الحَيا تَوارَت

جادَت بِالروحِ حينَ لاقَت
لا اِلتَفَتَت وَلا اِستَشارَت

Rising Moon

My soul won the love of my Beloved.
When I saw all the wine cups passed around,
I stretched out my hand to touch the nectar,
and my heart glowed bright in the light it found.
I drank. My soul was filled. I lost my weight.
Then, lifted up, I flew above the ground.
The Moon rose in the sky, in its brightness.
Ashamed, wanting to hide, the sun went down.
He gave himself with generosity,
spoke words to no one else, nor turned around.

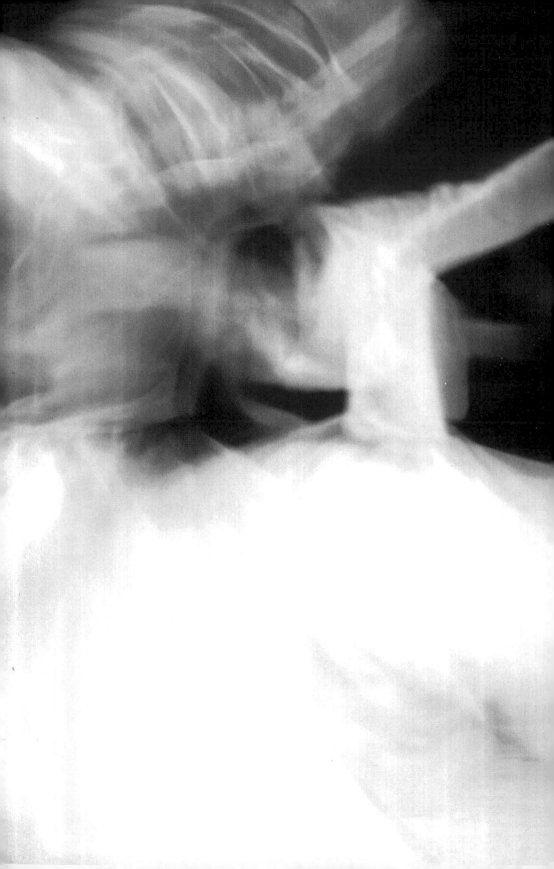

Cruel Rejection
الفرح المُرّ

الهجران

أُمسي وأُصبحُ بالجواء أتعذَّبُ
قَلبي على نَارِ الهوى يَتقلبُ

إن كنتَ تهجُرُني، تُهَذِّبُني بِهِ
أنتَ النُّهى وبَلاكَ لا أتهذَّبُ

مَا بَال قَلبِكَ قد قَسى؟ فَإلى مَتى
أَبكي ومِمَّا قَد جَرى أَتعتَّبُ

مِمّا أَحبُّ أَن اقولَ فَديتُكُم
أَحيى بِكُم وقَتيلَكُم اتلقَّبُ

وأشرتُمُ بالصَّبرِ لِي مُنَسلياً
مَا هَكذا عَشِقوا بِهِ، لا تَحسِبوا

مَا عِشتُ في هذا الفُراقِ سُويعَةُ
لَولا لَقاؤكَ كُلَّ يَوم أرقَبُ

إِني أَتوبُ مُناجِياً ومُنادِياً
فَأنا المُسيّ بِسيّدِي، والمُذنِبُ

تَبريزُ جَلَّ بِشمس دين سَيدِي
أَبكِي دَماً مِمّا جَنيتُ وأَشربُ

Separation

I woke from sleep tormented by love's fire,
tossing, turning on a bed of desire.
Have you abandoned me to make me pure?
I can't be pure without you, O Denier!
Why did you harden your heart that day?
When will I stop weeping and look higher?
My life? A sacrifice to you, I say.
I live in you and am your helpless prey.
I should accept this waiting, so you say.
But you should know that cannot be love's way.
No, I endured the absence of these years,
expecting each next moment you'd appear.
I have displeased my Master. That's my sin!
God glorified Tabriz with Shams ud-Din.
I repent, shouting, whispering my fears.
I cry tears of blood, and I drink my tears.

الحلم

هَيَّجَ نَومي ونَفَى رِيحٌ على الغَورِ هَفا
أذكَرَني وامِضُهُ طَيبَ زَمانٍ سَلَفا
يا رَشأً الحاظُهُ صَيَّرنَ رُوحي هَدَفا
يا قَمراً الفاظُهُ اورثنَ قَلبي شَرَفا
شَوَّقَني، ذَوَّقَني، أدرَكَني، أضحَكَني
أفقَرَني، اشكَرَني، صاحِبُ جُودٍ وعُلا
إذا حَدا طَيَّبَني وإن بَدا غَيَّبَني
وإن نَأى شَيَّبَني، لا زالَ يَومُ الملتقى
أكرِم بِحبي سامِياً، أضحى لِصيدٍ رَامِياً
حَتى رَمى بِأَسهُمٍ فيهِنَّ سَقمي وشِفا
يا قَمرَ الطَوارِقِ، تاجاً عَلى المَفارِقِ
لاحَ مِنَ المَشارِقِ، بَدَّلَ لَيلتي ضُحى
لاحَ مَفازُ حَسنٍ، يَفتح عَنها الوَسن
يا ثِقَتي لا تَهنوا واعتَجِلوا مُغتَنما
يا نَظري سَل، لِما غمَّضتَ عنهُ النَظَرا
أغضَبَهُ فاستَتَرا، عادَ إلى مَا لا يُرى
كُن دَنفاً مُقتَرباً مُمتَثِلاً مُضطَرِباً
مُنتَقِلاً مُغترِباً مِثلَ شَهابٍ في السَما
يا مَن يَرى ولا يُرى، زَالَ عَن العَينِ الكَرى
قَلبي عَشيقٌ لِلسَرى، فانتَهِضوا لِما ورا.

A Dream

Asleep: A storm blew through my emptiness,
reminding me of pleasures now long past.
You flashed your eyes. O Moon! They pierced my chest.
You spoke the words, and so my heart was blessed.
You filled me with desire, gave me a taste.
When you drew near, I smiled at your embrace.
A beggar, I gave thanks to be so base.
My master, you gave me your noble grace!
You sang to me at night: You taught me well.
You came: That was the end of me. I fell.
Then, when you left, my hair turned white as well.
We'll never part. Our union's here today.
Your love raised me so high, as just you may.
But when you came, I was your hunted prey.
You shot your arrow—you killed me that day.
That death was my cure and my salvation.
You're a Moon of bright stars! Crown on display,
you rose in the East, changed night into day.
A victory! I woke and saw my Lord!
My soul! Look up! and now take your reward.
My eyes! He's gone. You blinked, and he broke free.
He veiled his face in anger, ran from me.
I am a lover, sick with love, trembling—
a comet in the sky, a refugee.
You, the one who sees, whom I cannot see,
sleep left my eyes. My heart cannot be free.
And so, I yearn and wander the dark night.
I stay awake to find your mystery.

قصر الكمال

يا مَن بَنا قَصرَ الكَمالِ مُشيداً
لا زَالَ سَعداً*، بِالسُّعُودِ مُؤيداً
هَزَّ القُلوبَ وَرَدَّها بِصُدودِهِ
فَغذا دِماءُ العاشِقينَ مُبَدِداً
يا ساكِنَينَ مَحالَ العِشق في قلقٍ
تَظنُنونَ أَنَّ العِشق يَتركُكُم سُداً
لا وَالذي حَازَ المَلاحةَ والبَها
وَلَم يُبقِ لِلعُشاقِ حَيلًا ولا يداً
وَذَلِكَ شَمسُ الدين مَولًا وَسَيّداً
وَتَبريزُ مِنهُ كَالفَراديسِ قَد غَدا.

---

* . سُعُود النُّجوم: (الفلك) عدّة كواكب يُقال لكلّ واحد منها سَعْد كذا ومنها: سَعْد السُّعود وهو
أحدها، وسَعْد الذابح. سعد السعود في المَنْزِل الرَّابِعُ والعِشْرُونَ مِنْ مَنَازِلِ القَمَر

Palace of Perfection

You who built a palace of perfection,
Sa'd*—your star—still shines in its section,
upheld by Su'ud—stars that circle round.
You broke our hearts with your cruel rejection:
the blood of lovers flowed in sacrifice.
Look! all you waiting here. They paid the price.
His lovers cannot love and live in fear.
No! And, he didn't give us any choice.
I swear by his beauty, you're not alone.
That Shams, he's here—to guide and to entice.
Because of him, Tabriz is Paradise.

---

*Al-Su'ud is the traditional Arabic name of Beta Aquarii (β Aqr, β Aquarii), a double star in
the constellation Aquarius. The singular star in the group is called Sa'd, which also means luck.
Al-Sa'd al-su'ūd, the "luck of the lucky" is the brightest star in the group and served as one of the
stable anchor points by which other stars were charted.

ماذا ترى؟

فِيما تَرى؟ فِيما تَرى؟ يا مَن يَرى ولا يُرى
العَيشُ في اَكنافِنا والمَوتُ في اَركانِنا
إن تُدننا طُوبى لَنا، إن تُحفِنا يا وَيلَنا
يا نُورَ ضوءٍ ناظِراً، يا خاطِراً مُخاطِراً
نَدعوكَ رَبّاً حاضِراً في قَلبِنا تَفاخُراً
فكُن لَنا فِي ذُلِّنا بَرّاً، كَريماً، غافِراً.

What Do You See?

What do you see?
You who sees and whom I cannot see.
Life sits in my lap. Death stands by my side.
If you receive me, I am blessed.
If you reject me, I have lost my soul.
Like the dazzle of light,
a dangerous thought, you are.
Loving, generous, forgiving God!
You are here. You see my pride.
Be my abasement! Be my Savior!

نور الروح

يا مُنيرَ الغَدِ يا رُوحَ البَقا
يا مُجيرَ البَدرِ في كَبِدِ السمَّا
أنتَ رُوحُ الله في اوصافِهِ
أنتَ كَشَّافُ الغِطا، بَحرُ العَطا
تَقتُلُ العُشَّاقَ عَدلًا كامِلًا
ثُمَّ تُحييهم بِغَمزاتِ الرِّضى
صائدُ الأبطالِ مِن عينِ الظِّبا
مالِكُ المُلَّاكِ في رِقِّ الهوى
قَومُ عيسى لَو رَأوا إحياءَهُ
عَالَمَ الحِسِّ، أنكروا عيسى إذا
أينَ موسى؟ لو رَأى تِبيانَهُ
لَم يُواسِ الخِضرَ يَوماً كَمالًا
لَيتَ أبونا آدَمُ يَدري بِهِ
إذ نَأى مِن جَنةٍ، لِما بَكا
هَجرُهُ نارٌ هَوَينا قَعرَهُ
يا شَفيعاً، قُل لَنا أينَ الرَّدا؟
خَدُّهُ ناراً يُطفِئُ نارَنا
يُطفِئُ النيرانَ نارٌ، مَن رَأى!؟

Light of My Soul

Light of my soul! You're the source of life's spark!
My Lord! My Savior! Full moon through night's dark!
You, Spirit of God and Spirit of love!
Lift the veils, my generous Patriarch!
With perfect justice, you slay your lovers,
cut down a mighty hero with your sword.
A glance of your love and he recovers,
masters become slaves of love, at your word.
If they could see you bring the dead to life,
the Christians would abandon Jesus Christ.
If Moses had heard your wise oration,
would he waste time on Khidr's* advice?
I wish Adam had known you. He wept so
needlessly when cast out of Paradise.
You left us, and we fell into hellfire.
O Master! Soon, let death end my desire.
Make a fire to put out my fire.
Is there such thing? Fight fire with fire.

---

*Al-Khidr is believed to be a mythical saint who leads people to true knowledge. He is associated in Islamic traditions with Moses's quest for inner knowledge and wisdom.

العشق جاري

أكنتَ صاعِقةً يا حَبيبُ أو نَاراً
فَما تَركتَ لنا مَنزِلًا ولا دَاراً
بِكَ الفِخارُ ولكِن بُهيتُ مِن سكرٍ
فَلستُ أفهَمُ لَي مَفخَراً ولا عاراً
مَتى أتوبُ مِن الذَنبِ، تَوبتي ذَنبي؟!
مَتى أُجارُ إذا العِشقُ صارَ لي جاراً؟!
يَقولُ عَقلي لا تُبدِلَنَ هُدىً بردى
أما قَضيتَ بِهِ في هَلاكِ أوطاراً؟

Love Is My Savior

Were you a lightning bolt or just a ball of flame?
You left me with no home here, all the same.
I worship you, but drunk I here remain.
Is that your grace, or is it my soul's stain?
If I repent my sin, that's sin . . . and shame.
If love is my savior, so when will I be saved?
Now reason shouts at me: "No! Don't step off
the righteous path or it will be your grave!"
But isn't death the only thing I crave?

كان عيدا

أتاكَ عيدُ وِصالٍ فَلا تَذُقْ حُزنا
وِنلتَ خَيرَ رياضٍ، فَنِعمَ ما سَكَنا
وَزالَ عَنكَ فِراقٌ، أمَرُّ مِن صَبرٍ
وِمِحنةٍ فَتَنَتنا، خابَ مَن فُتِنا
فَهزَّ غُصنَ سُعُودٍ، وكُل مِن جَنا شَجرٍ
فَقرَّ عَينكَ مِنهُ، ونِعمَ ذاكَ جَنا
فَطِب، نَجوتَ مِن أصحابِ قَريةٍ ظَلَمَت
وَنَال قَلبك مِنهُم، شَقاوةً وَعَنا.

It Was a Celebration!

It was a celebration! Do not grieve!
He made me to lie down in green pastures.
That paradise, my home: I cannot leave.
Then, separation—bitter as aloe.
He's gone! Calamity has seduced me.
You know how sad the one seduced will be.
Still, I shook a branch from Love's tree. I ate
its blessed fruit. Eat your fill! What bounty!
I'm saved from those whose path does not run straight.
My heart before knew only pain and hate.

اوحشتنا

طَالَ مَا بِتنا بَلاكُمُ يَا كَرامي وشَتتنا
يَا حَبيبَ الرُّوحِ أَينَ المُلتَقى أوحَشتَنا
حَبّذا شَمسُ العُلى! مِن سَاعةٍ نَورتَنا
مَرحَباً بَدرُ الدُّجى، في لِيلةٍ أَدهَشتَنا
لَيسَ نَبغي غَيرَكُم، قَد طَالَ مَا جَرَّبتَنا
مَا لَنا مَولى سِواكُم، طَالَ مَا فَتَّشتَنا
يَا نَسيمَ الصُّبحِ إنّي عِندما بَشرتَني
يَا خَيالَ الوَصلِ رُوحي عِندَما جشمتنا
يَا فُراقَ الشَّيخِ شَمسِ الدينِ مِن تَبريزِنا
كَم تَرى في وَجهِنا آثارَ مَا حَرَّشتَنا؟

Longing

It's so long since I spent the night with you.
My friends! You know how we were torn apart.
Love of my soul, where will we meet again?
Noon Sun! I need your brightness in my heart.
Hey! Full Moon! Blinding light that stuns all men!
So long deserted, I want none but you.
Master! How long is it since you withdrew?
You were my Morning Breeze, who brought good news.
Seduce me now. Save me with love once more.
My Lord, my Shams al-Din, you've left my view.
On my face, see the damage that you do.

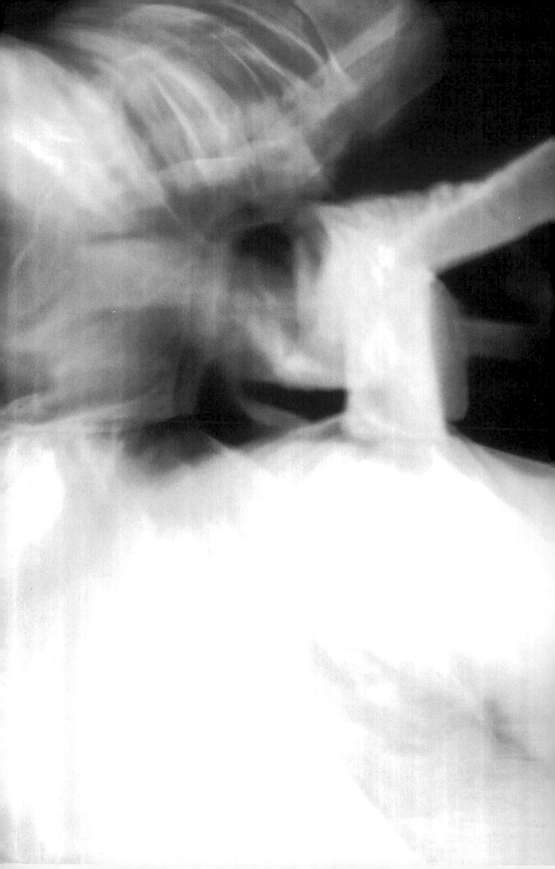

Good News!

البشارة السارة

تعال إلى دارنا

جاءَ الربيعُ مُفتخرا في جِوارِنا
جاءَ الحَبيبُ مُبتَسماً وَسَط دارِنا
طِيبُوا واكرِموا، وتَعالوا لِتشرَبوا
عِندَ الحَبيب مُبتشرا فِي عُقارِنا
مَن رامَّ مَغنَماً وتَصدى جوهراً
فليَلزم الجَوارى وَسَطَ بحارِنا.

Come to My House

Good news! Springtime came, and we saw it come.
My true lover just walked in—he's smiling.
Let's be pure, and let's be generous. Come!
Drink in the company of the Beloved.
Good news! He's here. So, come to my house. Come!
If you want true wealth, he will give you jewels.
Come! Stay near. Swim in this vast ocean. Come!

البشارة

وَرَدَ البَشيرُ مُبشراً بِبشارةٍ
أَحيى الفُؤادَ عَشيةً بِوجودِها
فكأنَّ أَرضاً نَورَت بِربيعِها
فكأنَّ شَمساً أَشرَقَت بِخُدودِها
يا طاعِني فِي صَبوَتي وتَهَتُّكي
اُنظُر إلى نارِ الهَوى وَوقُودِها.

Glad Tidings!

He came with glad tidings! He brought good news!
He raised the dead. Revived my heart's refuse.
He is spring! The desert blooms. Renewal!
He is the rising Sun! Lord of God's rule!
You blame me for my love and sinfulness?
See the flames of my love! He's their fuel.

صافية الخمر تضيء السماء

قَد اَشرَقَت الدُّنيا مِن نورٍ حُمَيّانا
البَدرُ غَدا سَاقي والكَأسُ ثُرَيانا
الصَبوةُ اِيماني والخَلوةُ بُستاني
وَالمَشجَرُ نُدماني والوَردُ مُحَيّانا
مَن كانَ لَهُ عِشقٌ، فَالمَجلِسَ مَثواهُ
مَن كانَ لَهُ عَقلٌ اِيّاهُ واِيّانا
مَن ضاقَ بِهِ دارُ، أو اَعطَشَهُ نَارُ
تَهدِيهِ إلى عَينٍ، يَسترجِعُ رَيّانا
مَن لَيسَ لَهُ عَينٌ، يستَبصِرُ عَن غَيبٍ
فَليَأتِ عَلى شوقٍ في خِدمَةِ مَولانا
يا دَهرُ سِوى صَدرِ شَمسِ الحَق تَبريزٍ
هَل اَبصَرَ في الدُّنيا، اِنسانُكَ اِنساناً
طُوبى لَكَ يا مَهدِي، قَد ذُبتَ مِنَ الجُهدِ
اعرَضتَ عَن الصُّورةِ كَي تُدرِكَ مَعنانا
مَن كانَ لَهُ هَمٌّ يُفنيهِ وَيُرديهِ
فَليشربَ وَليسكرَ مِن قَهوةِ مَولانا.

Your Wine Lights the World

The light of your pure wine will save the world!
Full Moon! Wine, in your cup of stars unfurled.
Love is my faith, solitude my station,
trees my companions, and flowers my friends.
If you're in love, join the congregation!
If you still have a mind, then stay away.
If you're pressed at home and parched by fire,
I'll take you to a secret stream I know.
You can drink, satisfy your desire—
and, if your eyes can't see what's hidden there,
just bring your thirst to serve our Messiah.
Centuries! Look! See the Sun of Tabriz!
Is there another being to admire?
Blessed Mahdi! You melted in fire—
you cast off the form, reached a Truth higher.
When troubles find you, bring you disaster:
Drink! Get high on the brew of our Master.

منهاج الطلب

السِلْمُ مِنهاجُ الطَلَب، الحِلمُ مِعراجُ الطَرَب
والنارُ صرافُ الذهب، والنورُ صرافُ الوَلا
العِشقُ مِصباحُ العَشا، والهَجرُ طَبّاخُ الحَشا
والوصلُ تِرياقُ الغشا، يا مَن على قلبي مَشا
الشَمسُ في أفراسِنا، والبِدَرُ مِن حُراسِنا
وَالعِشقُ مِن جُلاسِنا، مَن يَدرِ مَا في راسِنا؟
يا سائِلي عَن حُبِّهِ أكرِم بِهِ، انعِم بِهِ
كُلُّ المنى في جَنبِهِ، عِندَ التَجَلي كالهبا
يا سائِلي عَن قِصَني، العِشقُ قِسمي، حِصَتي
والسُكرُ أفنى غِصَتي، يا حَبَّذا لِي حَبَّذا
الفَتحُ مِن تُفاجِكُم، والحشرُ مِن أصباحِكُم
القَلبُ مِن أرواحِكُم، في الدَّورِ تِمثالُ الرَحا
أَرياحُكُم تُجلي البصر، يَعقُوبُكُم يُلقي النَظَر
يا يُوسُفينا في البَشر، جُودوا بِما الله اشترى
الشمسُ خَرَّت والقَمر، نُكِسا مَع الإحدى عشر
قَدَّامُكُم فِي يَقظةٍ، قُدامَ يُوسُفَ فِي الكَرى
أَصلُ العَطايا دَخلُنا، ذَخرُ البَرايا نَخلُنا
يا مَن لِحُبٍّ أو نَوى، يَشكو مَخالِبَ النوى.

Peace Is the Path

Peace is the path of search. Patience is enchantment to me.
With fire he tests the gold . . . with light he tests my loyalty.
Love, my lamp in darkness . . . and his absence cremates my heart.
Love's union is my cure, you crushed my very soul in me.
Your sun is my strong steed: the moon is my protector, too.
Love is my companion. Who knows what's in my fantasy?
You ask about his love: his gifts, his mercy, his favors.
My wishes, when he comes, they disappear like smoke for me.
You ask for my story: this passion is my destiny.
Drink erased my sorrow: this wine is good, so good for me.
Starting with the apple . . . the Day of Judgment is my dawn.
My heart springs from your soul, as from a turning potter's wheel.
Your breeze cures all blindness, and Jacob sees Joseph again.
You are my two Josephs. Be generous with God's bounty.
All planets bow to you: the sun, the moon are not shining.
Awake, I see you here, while Joseph saw you just in sleep.
Alms are my only wealth, my dates, the pride of all the land.
Why wail with love's desire? You're in the grip of love's bounty.

الجمال الغائب

يا خَفِيَّ الحُسنِ بَين النَاسِ يا نُورَ الدُجى
أنتَ شَمسُ الحَقِ تَخَفى بَين شَعشاع الضُحى
كادَ رَبُ العَرشِ يَخفي حُسنَهُ مَن نَفسِهِ
غِيرَةً مِنهُ عَلى ذاكَ الكَمالِ المُنتَهى
لَيتَني يَوماً اَخرُ مَيتاً في فَيِّه
إنَّ في مَوتي هُناكَ دَولةً لا تُرتَجى
في غُبارِ نَعلِهِ كُحلٌ يُجَلّي عن عَمى
في عُيونِ فَضلِهِ الوافي زِلالٌ للظما
غَيرَ أنَّ السَيرَ والنُقلانَ في ذاكَ الهَوى
مُشكِلٌ صَعبٌ مَخوفٌ، فيهِ اِهراقُ الدِمّا
نُورُهُ يَهدي إلى قَصرٍ رَفيعٍ آمِنٍ
لا أُبالي مِن ضَلالٍ فيهِ، لي هَذا الهُدى
أبشِري يا عَينِ مِن اِشراقِ نورٍ شامِلٍ
مَا عَليكِ مِن ضَريرٍ سَرمَدِيٌ لا يَرى
أصبَحت تَبريزُ عِندي قِبلةً أو مَشرِقاً
ساعةٌ أَضحى لِنورٍ، ساعةٌ أَبغى الصَلا
أيُها السَاقي أَدِر كَأسَ البَقا مِن حُبِهِ
طالَ مَا بِتنا مَريضاً نَبتَغي هَذا الشِفا
لا نُبالي مِن لَيالٍ شَيبتنا بُرهةً
بَعدَما صِرنا شبَاباً مِن رَحيقٍ دائماً
أيُها الصَاحونَ فِي أيامِهِ، تَعساً لَكُم
اِشرَبوا اِخوانَنا مِن كَأسِهِ، طُوبى لَنا
"حَصحَصَ الحَقُ الحَقيقُ المُستَضي مِن فَضلِه
سَوفَ يَهدي الناسَ من ظُلماتِهِم نَحو الفَضا
يا لَها مِن سُوءِ حَظً مُعرِضٍ عَن فَضلِهِ
مُنكِرٍ مُستكبِرٍ حَيران فِي وَادي الرَدى
مُعرِضٍ عَن عَينِ عَدلٍ مُستديمٍ للبَقا
طالِبٍ للماءِ في وَسواسِ يَومٍ لِلكَرى
عَينُ بَحرٍ فُجِرَت مِن أرضِ تَبريزٍ لَها
أرضُ تَبريزٍ فَداكِ رُوحُنا نِعمَ الثَّرى.

Hidden Beauty

Hidden Beauty! In the darkness, my sight!
You, ray of truth! You hide in morning's light.
God in glory! You almost hid yourself
from your own might, seeking full perfection.
I just want to die with you in sight,
to die there in a place above my right.
The dust beneath his feet will heal the blind.
His glance is rain for thirsty humankind.
But if you choose to walk his path of love,
you'll spill your blood, and troubles won't be kind.
His light will guide you to his high palace.
Don't doubt! This is the path of truth, of bliss.
My eyes rejoice to see his full light shine.
Forget the one who came before, sightless.
Tabriz is now the place I face to pray.
Sometimes, I am pure light! But not today.
Now, I want to bow down in simple prayer.
Wine boy! Hand round the cup of love, I say!
So long I was sick and needed this care!
Forget the nights that once whitened my hair.
I've found my youth again in this sweet wine.
If you're still sober now, then you're behind!
You're miserable, my brother, and how sad!
Drink from the hidden cup, and you will find
pure joy. His light will bring us truth. We're blessed!
He'll guide us from darkness toward a new day.
Pity the one who turns his face away.
So proud, lost in this valley of decay,
he scorns the river of justice flowing
with life his way and searches for water
in his dismay—afraid that death is near.
Rivers of water gush out from Tabriz.
Blessed Land! I give my soul for Tabriz.

علونا سماء الود

عَلونا سَماءَ الودِ مِن غَيرِ سُلَّمِ
وهَل يَهتَدي نَحو السماءِ الذَوائِبُ؟

ايَعلوا ظَلامُ الكَونِ نورُ وَدادِنا؟؟
وَقَد جاوَزَ الكَونين، هَذا عَجائِبُ

فَإن فارقَ الأيامَ بَينَ جُسومِنا
فَوالله إنَّ القَلبَ مَا هُو غائِبُ

فَقَلبيَ خَفيفُ الظعن نَحو أَحِبَّتي
وأن ثَقُلَت مِن ظعنهنَّ التَّرائِبُ

عَليكُم سَلامي مِن صَميمِ سَريرَتي
فَإنّي كَقَلبي أو سَلامِي لائِب

فَكَيفَ يَتوبُ القَلبُ عَن ذَنبِ وُدِّكُم
فَقَلبي مَدا عَمّا خَلاكُم لَنائِبُ

جَوابٌ لِمَن قَد قَالَ عَابِدُ بَعلَةٍ
أَرى البَعلَ قَد بَالت عَليهِ الثَّعالِبُ*

جَوابُ نَصيرِ الدّينِ لَيثُ فَضائِل
أَرَى الودَّ قَد بالَت عَليهِ الأَرانِبُ.

---

*. مستوحى من أبيات شعر قالها أبو ذر الغفاري حين رأي ثعلبا يبول على صنم كان يعبده

I Climbed to Heaven

Without a ladder, I climbed to heaven.
Calamities, can they find this heaven,
and dim the light of our love in heaven?
Look! Our love shines on, past earth and heaven!
The days have kept our bodies far apart,
I swear by God, my heart is still with you.
My heart is tender when my love is new,
sad and grieving when lovers then must part.
My heart sends you my messages of love—
no end. But I'm still thirsty! What to do?
My soul returns to places I saw you.
Can I repent the sin of love this true?
He says you're an idol that I worship,
can't see the fox piss on my graven god.*
Nasir al-Din!† He's the king of virtues!
No foxes, only rabbits piss on love.

---

*This refers to a poem by Abu Thar al-Ghafari, an early convert to Islam, that he wrote after he saw a fox urinating on an idol he worshiped at the time.

†Nasir al-Din al-Tusi was a Muslim scholar and a contemporary of Rumi.

بُشرى

فَدَيتُكَ يا ذا الوَحي آياتُهُ تَترى
تُفَسِّرُها سِرّاً وتَكنى بِها جِهراً
وانشَرتَ اَمواتا واَحييتَهُم بِها
فَدَيتُكَ مَا اَدراك بِالاَمرِ مَا اَدري
فَعادوا سُكارى في صِفاتِكَ كُلَّهُم
وَمَا طَعِموا اِثماً وَمَا شَربوا خَمراً
ولَكِن بَريقُ القُربِ اَفنى عُقُولَهُم
فَسُبحانَ من اَرسى وَسُبحانَ من اَسرى
سَلامٌ على قَومٍ تُنادي قُلوبُهُم
بِالسِنَةِ الاَسرارِ شُكراً لَهُ شُكراً
فَطُوبى لَمن اَدلى من الجَدِّ دَلوه
وفي الدَّلوِ حُسناً، يوسفُ قالَ: يا بشرى
يُطالِعُ في شُعشاعِ وَجنَةِ يُوسفٍ
حَقائقُ اَسرارٍ يُحيطُ بِها خُبراً
تَجلّى عَليه الغَيبُ واندَكَّ عَقلُهُ
كَما اندَكَّ ذَلَّكَ الطورُ واستَهدَمَ الصَخرا
فَظَلَ غَريقُ العِشقِ روحاً مُجَسماً
وَنوراً عَظيماً لَم يَذِر دونَهُ سَتراً.

Good News!

Now, I will sacrifice my life for you!
You hear the secret verses and give them
meaning too. We all see you take their names,
raise the dead with those verses, make them new.
Now, I will sacrifice my life for you!
How did you learn the mysteries you knew?
Risen from the grave, drunk on your beauty—
without a sip of sinful wine, askew.
A glimpse of your nearness drove them all mad.
Blessed are they! You shelter them near you.
Blessed at dawn when they go on their way.
Peace be upon the people of the heart
whose tongues keep secrets. Give thanks. Thanks! I say.
Praise be! With their noble deeds they prove his sway.
Then, Joseph shouts: "Good news! Their proof is true."
I see Joseph's face in radiant light.
The secrets have appeared now, in plain sight,
his mind destroyed, and reason put to flight,
Mt. Sinai crushed, stone tablets smashed with might.
Like them, he's drowned in love and brilliant light,
a piercing light no veil will dim this night.

يوم التناد

مَن رَأى دُرًّا تَلَألأً نُورُهُ وَسَط الفُؤاد؟

بَيننا وَبينهُ قَبلَ التَجلّي اَلفَ واد

جاء مَن يُحيي المَواتَ والرَميمَ والرَفات

أَيُها الأمواتُ قُومُوا وابصِروا يَومَ التَناد

طارَتِ الكُتبُ الكِرامُ مِن كِرام كاتِبين

ايقِظوا مِن غَفلَةٍ ثُمَّ انشُروا للاجتِهاد

جاءَنا مِيزانُنا كَي نَختَبِر اوزانَنا

رَبنا أَصلِح شَأنَنا أو جُد بِعَفوٍ با جَواد

اِضحَكوا بَعدَ البُكا، يَا نِعمَ هَذا المُشتَكا

قَد خَرجتم مِن حِجابٍ وانتبهتُم مِن رُقاد.

Judgment Day

You saw the jewel that glowed inside my heart?
A thousand river beds kept us apart.
But he appeared and gave the Day its start.
And then, he stirred the dust and raised the dead.
You corpses! Rise and see his Day of Dread!
Thrown out the learned books and all they said.
Wake up! Run! Find new meanings in the Law.
He is the scale: Now he will weigh each flaw.
He is generous! Stop weeping and laugh!
God hid our sins, forgave us all he saw.
Praise to his judgment! He cast off your veils!
Then, wake from your dark sleep and gaze in awe.

APPENDIX

The Arabic poems in this book are taken from *Kulliyat Shams ya Divan-e Kabir*, edited by Badi-u-Zaman Furuzanfar (Tehran: Amir Kabir Press, 1957). All the poems, with the exception of the last poem, are in volume one. The last poem, "Judgment Day," is in volume two. The corresponding numbers of each of the poems and lines in Faruzanfar's manuscript are listed below. For example, "(269: 3036–38)" refers to poem number 269, lines 3036 through 3038 in Furuzanfar's volume.

Leave Behind Temptation
"Let's Be Pure" (269: 3036–38)
"Rejoice in Silence" (320: 3480–85)
"Banner of Love" (282: 3140–46)
"I Fell in Love with Angels" (287: 3112–18)
"He Stole My Heart!" (284: 3150–54)

You Sang of Love
"You Sang of Love, So We Came" (276: 3048–58)
"The Price of Love" (277: 3103–11)
"Drunken Brothers" (289: 3177–80)
"This Eye" (109: 1228–29)
"He's Never Bored with Love" (270: 3036–42)
"What Happened to Me?" (375: 3069–87)
"Have Mercy!" (288: 3167–76)

Come, Let's Pray
"We're All Drunk" (217: 3043–47)
"Come, Let's Pray!" (281: 3134–39)
"Night Visitors" (274: 3064–68)

"The Cupbearer Will Explain" (279: 3119–24)
"Rising Moon" (517: 5519–23)

   Cruel Rejection

"Separation" (319: 3472–79)
"A Dream" (266: 3001–10)
"Palace of Perfection" (286: 3159–63)
"What Do You See?" (262: 2966–68)
"Light of My Soul" (280: 3125–33)
"Love Is My Savior" (218: 2467–70)
"It Was a Celebration!" (285: 3155–58)
"Longing" (273: 3059–63)

   Good News!

"Come to My House" (283: 3147–49)
"Glad Tidings!" (287: 3164–66)
"Your Wine Lights the World" (267: 3011–18)
"Peace Is the Path" (33: 444–48)
"Hidden Beauty" (276: 3088–3102)
"I Climbed to Heaven" (318: 3464–71)
"Good News!" (268: 3019–27)
"Judgment Day" (1010: 10655–59)